THE SIGNS OF
JESUS'
DEITY
IN THE GOSPEL OF JOHN

REVISED EDITION

SOLOMON E. FIELDS

ISBN 978-1-957943-87-9 (paperback)
ISBN 978-1-957943-88-6 (hardcover)
ISBN 978-1-957943-89-3 (digital)

For more information, email: drsolomon@anchored4jesus.com

Printed in the United States of America

ENDORSEMENTS

"I thank Dr. Fields for presenting such a fresh view on the Signs (miracles) of Jesus. These Signs are a testament of the Divine powers of his attributes shown to man during His ministry here on earth. No one else within the historical times of man on earth could possibly exhibit these things except the Son of God.

Being a student of history, I appreciated the book's use of the Old Testament to give strength to the acts rendered by our Lord Jesus Christ. The Old Testament connection expounds on the fact that the Word (Jesus) was preexistent from the beginning, as indicated in the first verse of the Book of John. The Word was God prior to the beginning, and so, in essence, these powers of Signs existed before the beginning.

Again, thank you, Dr. Fields, for this persuasive view on the Signs of Jesus, it is a good resource for study. I will recommend the book for my students."

Dr. Bill Odems, Mount Olive Bible Institute, Austin, TX

"Whether you are a pastor, minister, or layperson, you will find this in-depth exposition of the miracles of Jesus, as chronicled in the Gospel of John, to be inspirational, insightful, and provocative. The meticulous examination and brilliant writing of Dr. Fields reinforce the truth regarding the deity of Jesus as The Christ."

Cory S. Powell, Pastor, New Dimensions Tabernacle, Lubbock, TX.

"Who do you say Christ is? Dr. Solomon Fields provides commentary and research about the seven miracles of Jesus and other signs to examine doctrinal beliefs. More importantly, Fields provides insight and inspiration by offering an analysis of related scripture to assert and affirm the unambiguous and non-negotiable truth about the deity of Christ. Be it individual or small group Bible studies; this book is a great resource for teachers, clergy, or anyone seeking to share the wonderful news that Jesus Christ is the anointed one of God."

Amanda Banks, Ph.D., Lubbock, TX

PREFACE

This research project will examine the signs recorded in the gospel of John and explore whether they provide definitive proof of the deity of Jesus Christ. The study will analyze the background of the audience during the time of Jesus and that of the implied readers of the gospel of John, which is inclusive of the early church fathers and the present-day audience.

There has been a lot written on the social culture of the Mediterranean people and their anticipation of the Messiah in respect to the gospel of John. This study will aim to explain the text in John's gospel, specifically regarding those passages related to the traditional seven signs and the other nontraditional miraculous signs. I will analyze the acceptance or lack of acceptance of the signs that John incorporates in the gospel as reasons for believing in Jesus Christ, the Son of God. The project will also consider the post-resurrection perspective of the uniqueness of the signs within the early church and the present-day church concerning the Christian faith.

I endeavor to provide a concise resource tool for those who minister through preaching, teaching, and leading Bible studies in their discussion of the signs within the gospel of John. Our objective is to provide a supplemental tool to the *Holy Bible* and other research material that will briefly clarify and analyze the miracles from the viewpoint of the audience and potential reader in ascertaining John's purpose in writing the gospel. We do not intend to survey all of the vast material written on John or debate the numerous theories regarding the authorship and the Johannine community. Therefore, this project will concur with the traditional conservative assumption of John, the son of Zebedee, being the author of the fourth gospel.

Our focus is to give honor and glory to the Lord Jesus Christ so that souls may be saved and strengthened in the kingdom of God.

TABLE OF CONTENTS

CHAPTER 1

Introduction

General Overview

Numerous books, commentaries, journals, and articles are available on the gospel of John, from the prologue of chapter 1 through the epilogue of chapter 21. Within verses 1:19 to 12:50 of what Kostenberger calls the Book of Signs, there are many indicators of supernatural or divine authority within the narrative events described by the author.[1] The author of the fourth gospel states that Jesus performed other signs that were visibly evident to His disciples; however, John incorporated these specific signs in his writing to solicit belief that "Jesus is the Christ, the Son of God, and that believing you may have life in His name" (John 20:31). The gospel's author does not specifically state the number of signs within the gospel, nor does he stress the chronological order after the second sign of the healing of the nobleman's son in John 4:46–54. Our study will concentrate on whether these signs individually or collectively

---

[1] Andreas J. Kostenberger, *John: Baker Exegetical Commentary on the New Testament* (Grand Rapids, MI: Baker Academic, 2004), vii.

make a definitive case for the deity of Jesus Christ as the Son of God and therefore justify belief in Him. This project will examine each sign at its face value, analyze the reaction of the immediate audience to the signs, and determine whether there is strong support that something beyond the normal had taken place to prompt the audience and the future reader to believe in the deity of Jesus Christ, Son of God. Whether the immediate audience saw a relationship between the abnormal event and the intervention of divinity is questionable, and we will discuss it further in the subsequent chapters. Furthermore, we will consider the unique aspect of each sign and the impact it had upon the immediate audience, the early church, and the present-day church.

Research Background

There is a vast amount of research on the social aspect of the intended audience and those witnessing the signs performed by Jesus. The intended audience's theories range from unbelieving to believing Jews, Diaspora Jews, Gentiles and Christians in the Johannine community, and possibly those influenced by Gnosticism. Keener states that "although the author shows his knowledge of Judean and Jerusalem topography, the implied reader's knowledge appears to be more limited to Galilean sites emphasized in the traditional Gospel story known to us in the Synoptics."[2] In other words, the intended audience must have some background knowledge of Jewish culture and Galilean topology to decipher the meaning of the language. Carson also advocates a position that the gospel of John is evangelistic writing aimed at Jews and Jewish proselytes due to the language used insinuating Old Testament things such as the snake in the desert

---

[2] Craig S. Keener, *The Gospel of John* (Grand Rapids, MI: Baker Academic, 2003), 143.

(3:14) and manna from heaven (6:31).[3] I agree that the intended audience may not be exclusively a Judean audience but might suggest a theory of the gospel's intent at a diverse population. So the question remains whether the immediate audience and the future readers have enough information and aptitude to understand what these signs meant and prompt belief in the deity of Jesus Christ, the Son of God.

The issue of whether the attending audience in John's gospel was primarily Jews with the possible exception of the nobleman in John 4:46–54 is debatable. Bultmann proposes that the healing of the nobleman in John's gospel is based upon the healing of the centurion's son in Matthew 8:5–13 and Luke 7:1–10.[4] In some facets, Jesus's rebuke of the nobleman mirrors that given to the Syrophoenician woman in Mark 7:24–30. However, Carson contends that, unlike the centurion in Matthew 8:5–13 and Luke 7:2–10, nothing in John 4:46 suggests the royal official was a Gentile.[5] Therefore, we will surmise that many of the signs performed by Jesus in the Johannine writing were primarily in the presence of Jews, especially considering Edersheim's position that Jesus, as a Jew, spoke primarily to Jews.[6] Fredriksen does suggest the possibility of Diaspora Jews and Gentiles being present based upon archaeological studies of "many ossuaries (bone boxes used in secondary burial)" in Palestine with the names of the deceased in Greek.[7] However, we cannot make an absolute statement that John's gospel only has miracles performed in the presence of Jews.

[3] D. A. Carson, *The Gospel According to John* (Grand Rapids, MI: Eerdmans Publishing, 1991), 91.

[4] Rudolf Bultmann, *The Gospel of John: A Commentary*, trans. G. R. Beasley-Murray (Philadelphia: Westminster Press, 1971), 204.

[5] Carson, *The Gospel According to John*, 234.

[6] A. Edersheim, *The Life and Times of Jesus the Messiah*, vol. 1 (New York: Longmans, Green, and Co. 1896), xii–xiii.

[7] Paula Fredriksen, *Jesus of Nazareth, King of the Jews: A Jewish Life and the Emergence of Christianity* (New York: Alfred A. Knopf, 1999), 156.

I am aware of sign narratives within the Synoptic Gospels involving Gentiles; however, I will delimit this study and focus on those signs within John's writing and whether they can provide definitive proof of the deity of Jesus Christ. This study will examine the background aspects of the attending audiences in the narratives of the signs and address whether the implied audiences needed Jewish or biblical knowledge to prompt belief in the deity of Jesus Christ, Son of God. This study is important in today's use of the gospel in Christian ministry, as some clergy encourage newborn believers to read and study John's gospel before other books in the canon to reinforce their faith. For this reason, we must also briefly address the type of document John was writing: an evangelism tool, a means of Christian development, or an attempt to combat false doctrines during that period. Once again, the type of document written does not overshadow the purpose expressed in 20:31 regarding prompting belief in Jesus Christ as the Son of God.

Research Concern

The nucleus of this project is to study the individual and collective group of signs concerning satisfying John's purpose (20:31), regardless of whether a person was in the immediate audience or a future reader of the gospel. When studying the sign narratives, it is debatable whether each sign has sufficient evidence to stand exclusively on merit. Therefore, I will examine the signs in John's gospel from an individual and a collective perspective regarding their uniqueness and possibly divine intervention to determine whether they support a position of the deity of Jesus Christ and warrant faith in Him.

The resurrection of Jesus Christ is the ultimate sign pointing toward His deity. However, the research challenges regarding the early church and the present-day church will be in determining whether these signs, inclusive of the resurrection of Jesus, are sufficient to claim His deity. A study of the sign passages will also permit us to address the social, religious, and theological factors that impacted the attending audience's belief in Jesus and determine whether similar factors influenced belief by the early and later church.

Delimitations

Considering the surplus of material written on the gospel of John and, in particular, the signs therein, certain topics must remain beyond the scope of this project. We will not attempt to address the ongoing debate on whether the fourth gospel is a literary dependent of material from the Synoptic writers. Nor will this project attempt to review all of the Synoptic literature on the signs of the deity of Jesus Christ and their impact upon the church. Our analysis of the sign narratives in John's gospel will focus solely on the uniqueness of the signs and how they impacted the audience and the future reader in terms of satisfying John's purpose in 20:31.

Assumptions

I desire that this project benefits the body of Christ, and in particular, pastors, teachers, and lay members. The intent is to close the gap in knowledge and understanding of the relationship between the signs recorded in John's gospel and the deity of Jesus Christ. For this study, I have assumed that Christians believe that the Bible is the infallible and inerrant written Word of God, which expresses the truth of God's nature.[8] I have likewise assumed that the Bible is a reliable set of historical records of various events throughout the earthly life of Jesus. Bauckham writes about the historical Jesus, "For

---

[8] Charles Hodge, *Systematic Theology*, Vol. 1 (Peabody, MA: Hendrickson Publishers, 2008), 15.

Christian faith, this Jesus, the earthly Jesus as we can know him, is the Jesus of the canonical Gospels, Jesus as Matthew, Mark, Luke and John recount and portray him."[9] Therefore, I will concur that the historical Jesus is a fact and is the same as the theological Jesus of the Christian faith.

Procedural Overview

The process for determining whether these signs provide definitive proof of the deity of Jesus Christ will begin with a literature discussion in chapter 2, followed by chapters examining the traditional seven signs. Chapters 3 through 9 will examine and analyze the sign narratives in John's gospel, focusing on the uniqueness of the signs and the factors impacting the audience's understanding and belief in Jesus Christ, the Son of God. Chapter 10 will discuss the debatable signs, and then chapter 11 will cover the ultimate sign—the resurrection of Jesus Christ. Chapter 12 will outline the conclusions drawn from the study with a declaratory statement regarding whether these signs provide definitive proof of the deity of Jesus Christ.

The study will consider whether there were social, religious, and theological factors that influenced the audience's understanding or whether it was a deliberate rejection on a spiritual level. I will also examine the authentication of signs and whether John's signs are unique in terms of their relationship to other signs in the Synoptics and ancient history. We will agree with Keener that "ancient writers and storytellers often used miraculous works to authenticate deities or, more often, persons. Such signs demonstrated that the person

---

[9]   Richard Bauckham, *Jesus and the Eyewitnesses: The Gospels as Eyewitness Testimony* (Grand Rapids, MI: Eerdmans Publishing, 2006), 2.

indeed possessed the numinous authority to justify his (in the vast majority of cases, they were men) or her claims."[10]

Let us now consider a literature review of signs within the fourth gospel. This study will utilize databases such as texasgroup.worldcat. org, lubbocklibrary.com; logos.com; and Hunter Theological Library (EBSCOhost research) with access to various other search engines across the country. Theologians such as Carson, Michaels, Keener, Smith, Witherington, Neyrey, Kostenberger, Maline and Rohrbaugh, Grudem, Backham, Erickson, and many others will often be referenced in this project.

---

[10] Keener, *The Gospel of John*, 272.

CHAPTER 2

Literature Review

Audience Background

The historical setting of a person's surroundings and background experiences will shape their ideas and beliefs. Such was the case for the audience during Christ's miracles and the early and latter church. Today, we have a vast number of theologians who have written about the historic background of the audience during the time of Jesus Christ and the Johannine community during the first and second centuries after Christ. Factors involving the social-political climate and the religious background of the Jews could all potentially impact the audience's decision concerning the signs. Edersheim contends that the Holy Land was "a country of mixed and hostile races, of divided interests, were close by the side of the narrowest and most punctilious Pharisaism heathen temples rose, and heathen rites and customs openly prevailed."[11]

---

[11] A. Edersheim. *Sketches of Jewish Social Life in the Days of Christ* (London: The Religious Tract Society, n.d.), 20–21.

The Israelites' primary language of Hebrew changed to an Aramaean dialect except in the public worship and the learned academies of theological doctors due to the influx of heathen beliefs and values that pushed their way throughout the community. "Such words and names in the gospels as Raka, Abba, Golgotha, Gabbatha, Akel-Dama, Bartholomaios, Barabbas, Bar-Jesus, and the various verbal quotations, are all Aramæan."[12] The Jesus of Nazareth was a Jew who spoke Aramaean instead of Greek, with an initial focus of His ministry toward the Jews. It is reasonable to conclude that His Aramaean language would touch the Jews' intellectual and religious consciousness regarding understanding while spiritually expanding His teaching for all humankind.[13] Witherington suggests that John's audience was primarily Gentile based upon many explanatory remarks within the gospel. He concludes that John preached to a primarily Gentile audience that needed explanation of various terms.[14] Keener disagrees with Witherington's position and argues that the Diaspora Jews two decades after the temple's destruction, alone with the Gentiles, would need explanatory remarks.[15] The explanatory remarks by John do not necessitate a specific audience type in terms of Jew versus Gentile. Still, they could be the result of John's writing style and factors within his environment. In John 4:36–37, Jesus spoke of the Samaritans coming to Him by using a metaphor of the harvest season. John's explanatory comments could just as easily have been word prompts to assist the early church in understanding the events described.

Smith advocates Hellenism and Gnosticism (salvation through knowledge, primarily knowledge of one's heavenly origin) as influencing factors within the Johannine community to accept

---

[12] Ibid.

[13] Edersheim, *The Life and Times of Jesus the Messiah*, xii–xiii.

[14] Ben Witherington III, *John's Wisdom: A Commentary on the Fourth Gospel*, (Louisville, KY: Westminster John Knox Press, 1995), 32–35.

[15] Keener, *The Gospel of John*, 155.

or reject the Jesus of Nazareth.[16] Keener concurs that Hellenistic influence greatly impacted the culture of early Judaism.[17] There seems to be an integration of Judaic and Hellenistic cultures within the audience. Their preconceptions and doctrinal beliefs could weigh on the decision to recognize the miracles as signs of the deity of Jesus Christ. The religious beliefs also significantly helped shape the audience's opinion of the signs performed by Jesus. The predominance of the Pharisees' influence characterized this period to the extent that the people were required to adhere to the precepts of the scriptural Torah and obey the oral law, which included innumerable details that the common people were mandated to observe to achieve salvation.[18] Schurer states that "this exaggerated legalism had obtained such an absolute ascendency over the minds of the people, that all other tendencies were put entirely in the background."[19] When we combine this zealousness for the law alongside the anticipation of a Messiah, we cannot help but imagine the audience's mindset while Jesus is performing these miracles.

On the one hand, the Jewish leaders persecuted Jesus because of His noncompliance to the Sabbath Day (John 5:16, 9:16). Still, on the other hand, the common people elevated Jesus to be a prophet and king (John 6:14–15, 7:40–41). This study will investigate some specific factors that influenced and shaped the audience's decision in respect to acceptance or rejection of Jesus and whether these signs were sufficient to justify faith in the deity of Jesus Christ.

---

[16] Smith, *The Theology of the Gospel of John*, (Cambridge: University Press, 1995), 10–13.

[17] Keener, *The Gospel of John*, 155.

[18] E. Schürer, *A History of the Jewish People in the Time of Jesus Christ, first division*, Vol. 1, (Edinburgh: T&T Clark, 1890), 2.

[19] Ibid.

Purpose of Signs

Signs within the Old Testament were indicators of the presence of God or the assurance of His promises. Various Old Testament characters requested signs, such as Abram, who requested assurance of how he would know God had given him the land (Genesis 15:8); Moses, who was given three signs in Exodus 4:1–9 to let the children of Israel know that the God of Abraham, Isaac, and Jacob had appeared to him; and Gideon, who asked for three signs to confirm that God would use him to save Israel from the Midianites (Judges 6:12–40). Old Testament signs such as Noah and the rainbow or Elijah and fire from heaven show that these signs were supernatural indicators of the presence of God and confirmation of His word. The impact of individuals' beliefs in the Word of God and of His agents' conveying precious promises are illustrated in the Old Testament. Keener states that ancient signs generally authenticated the miracle worker, his teaching, and his authority.

Interestingly, the Jewish audience in the fourth gospel would request signs (2:18) and then blatantly reject them as an indication of the divine presence of God. Keener suggests that the signs in Luke-Acts are more authentic. In contrast, John's gospel signs perform an ambiguous function, almost hidden to those who are unworthy of following Jesus Christ.[20] Furthermore, why did the early church and even the present-day church accept these visible tokens as signifying the divine presence of God in the flesh? Perhaps to help the discussion, we need to look closer at the misunderstanding of signs witnessed by the audience.

---

[20] Ibid., 275.

Misunderstanding the Signs

It is amazing how two or more individuals can view the same sign and draw different conclusions. An event that can appear as a supernatural phenomenon can be rather complex when considering the miracle's relationship to the referent; the collection of other related miracles; and the interpreters' cultural, religious, and ideological views.[21] Malina and Rohrbaugh suggest that the reason for much of the misunderstanding is due to the world of John's gospel and the social system.[22] "Antilanguage is the language of an 'antisociety,' that is 'a society that is set up within another society as a conscious alternative to it. It is a mode of resistance, resistance which may take the form either of passive symbiosis or of active hostility and even destruction (Halliday 1978:171).'"[23] The misunderstanding of signs incorporates many factors of which "antilanguage" and "antisociety" could be influences; however, the reaction of the audience mentioned in passages such as John 5:16 and 7:31–32 suggests that other conditions and priorities are prompting the rejection of Jesus Christ as Son of God.

The historical background of the audience has a direct impact on their understanding of the signs within John's gospel. The audience believed many events were miracles because of supernatural intervention. Keener cites several miracles, such as the healing attributed to Vespasian and prayers answered for Hanina ben Dosa, whose reputation was so great that many believed that all the miracle workers were gone when he died.[24] Keener even writes of pagan miracles that showed up in third-century literature but then

---

[21] Millard J. Erickson, *Christian Theology,* 3rd ed. (Grand Rapids, MI: Baker Academic, 2013), 110.

[22] Bruce J. Malina and Richard L. Rohrbaugh, *Social-Science Commentary on the Gospel of John* (Minneapolis: Fortress Press, 1998), 3.

[23] Ibid., 7.

[24] Keener, *The Gospel of John,* 273.

acknowledged that these miracles could be attributed to similar Christian events.[25] The Jewish viewpoint of miracles attributed healings to God as opposed to medicine. Harvey argues that there was not an abundance of miracles during Jesus's ministry and none parallel to those Jesus performed. Furthermore, he advocates that the Jewish writings during this period show little interest in healing and exorcisms.[26]

> Honi and Haninah ben Dosa were perhaps exceptional intercessors rather than healers, exorcists, or miracle workers, and the phrase "men of the deed" itself (the class of men which is said to have ceased when Haninah died) can be shown not necessarily, or even probably, to refer to miracles.[27]

When reconsidering this study's definition of signs, the work of power or miracle must be a visible token indicating the identity of Jesus Christ, Son of God. Nicodemus attempted identifying Jesus in his testimony of the divinity of His signs in John 3:2b: "Rabbi, we know that You are a teacher come from God; for no one can do these signs that You do unless God is with him." Nicodemus links the signs of Jesus to the power of God but fails to complete the identification of Jesus's association with the Father. In essence, Nicodemus misunderstands the signs and views Jesus as a teacher instead of being the Son of God. In John 9:32–33, the Pharisees heard the testimony of the man who was born blind: "Since the world began it has been unheard of that anyone opened the eyes of one who was born blind. If this Man were not from God, He could do nothing." Kostenberger reminds us that the healing of blind people

---

[25] Ibid., 255.

[26] Anthony Ernest Harvey, *The Journal of Theological Studies* 54, no. 2 (Publication Type: Review, 2003), 664–666.

[27] Ibid.

was limited in the Old Testament and exceedingly rare in the Jewish tradition, according to the Tobit 11:10–14; cf. 2:10.[28]

I believe we can conclude that the healing of the man born blind is without parallel in Jewish history. This miracle provoked the Jewish leaders to pursue Sabbath Day violations against Jesus instead of considering Him as Christ. Nevertheless, the man born blind progresses in his faith. He recognizes Jesus as coming from God but again falls short in understanding the real identity until Jesus reveals Himself in John 9:35–38. Witherington suggests that we must be careful jumping the gun and assuming that the confession and prostration of the man is an indicator of full faith in Jesus Christ, especially since the death and resurrection had not occurred yet.[29]

At this point, the previously blind man worshipped Jesus, and then we are told nothing more about his life. However, we cannot ignore the fact that when this man learned that the identity of his healer was the Son of God, he believed and worshipped Him (John 9:35–38). We could ask the question, if this man realized the identity of Jesus Christ, Son of God, did he become a disciple and follow Jesus? Is this act of worship by the man definitive proof of the deity of Jesus Christ? The audience's reaction recorded in the Scriptures suggests that Jesus's signs were unique. Still, the uniqueness of the signs opens the door for misunderstanding of these visible tokens of divine revelation.

When considering the Jews' religious background in understanding the signs, the gospel of John indicates a direct relationship of the signs as being the divine authority from God the Father through His Son, Jesus Christ (John 20:31). The Jewish audience believed there was one God (monotheism), and this belief was taught from the Old Testament forward. The implication of polytheism was considered sinful and made the blasphemer subject to death. So in the discourse with the Jews after the man's healing

---

[28] Kostenberger, 292.

[29] Witherington, *John's Wisdom*, 184.

at the pool of Bethesda, Jesus used vague language that implies a direct relationship with the Father (5:17–18). However, due to their monotheistic background in theology, this concept of Jesus's being deity was an unacceptable doctrine, and they would choose any label for Jesus except the Son of God.

Much of the dialogue among Jesus, the disciples, and the Jews encompasses the language of a sage. During this period in history, Sages would advocate health, long life, and prosperity in abundance for those who follow the advice. Witherington contends "that sages in their advice were much concerned about good health and wellness (cf. Sir 25), which may explain why Jesus seems to have styled himself a physician (cf. Mk. 2:17 and Lk. 4:23) and was frequently found healing people."[30] Jesus's use of fragments from the Wisdom Literature contributed to the misunderstanding of the signs that should have pointed the audience to the identity of Jesus. The elusiveness and ambiguity of Jesus's responses are seen in the dialogue with His mother in John 2:4: "Woman, what does your concern have to do with Me?" After what present-day readers may consider a brush-off response, Jesus proceeds to turn water into wine. Another example of ambiguity is seen in the response of Jesus to the nobleman in John 4:46–50, whereby Jesus appears to rebuke him and then heals his sick son without satisfying the nobleman's request to travel to Capernaum. And another is found in the intentional healing of the man at the pool of Bethesda on the Sabbath after asking him, "Do you want to be made well?" (John 5:1–15). It would appear in the above dialogues involving the signs that Jesus intentionally asked probing questions or gave responses to assess the requestor, as opposed to just responding to clarify His ultimate intention. In addition to the elusive language, the audience's response in many of the sign narratives show their labeling Jesus with titles such as Rabbi or teacher (John 3:2); a prophet and a man (John 4:19, 29; 6:14); a

---

30 Ben Witherington III, *The Jesus Quest: The Third Search for the Jew of Nazareth*, 2nd ed. (Downers Grove, IL: InterVarsity Press, 1997), 191.

man called Jesus (9:11), a prophet (9:17); Lord, Christ, and Son of God (11:27); and teacher (11:28). The fact that Martha calls Jesus "Lord, Christ and Son of God" but then tells her sister, Mary, "the Teacher has come," shows the type of misunderstanding of who Jesus is by even His followers.

The Jewish leaders consistently expressed a misunderstanding regarding identifying Jesus; however, their position is more coupled to religious biases, social and economic status, and political relations with Rome. There is a blatant misunderstanding of the Pharisees in their response to Jesus in John 9:40–41. Michaels states, "Jesus can tell these Pharisees, 'Your sin remains' simply on the basis of what he views as their pretension to 'see,' and their consequent unwillingness to do what the man born blind has just done."[31] The misunderstanding of the sign of the healing of the man born blind is purely choice and not due to elusive language; in essence, it was not a misunderstanding on the Pharisees but simply a rejection of Jesus Christ.

Authentication of Signs

The definitions of *miracles* and *signs* are closely related; however, a sign will specifically point beyond the visibility of the supernatural toward the manifestation of something or someone else. In the case of the Johannine signs, John advocates that they point to the deity of Jesus Christ. Mark 6:5–6 suggests that the people, particularly those in Nazareth (and I believe other areas likewise), did not believe in miracles and therefore did not witness signs.

In the period of the Diaspora, there were many stories of healing activities and especially Jewish magicians. An example is seen in Acts 8:17–24 when Simon, a sorcerer, wanted the gift of laying hands on

---

[31] J. Ramsey Michaels, *The Gospel of John* (Grand Rapids, MI: Eerdmans Publishing, 2010), 575–576.

people and empowering them with the Holy Spirit. Keener argues that Jesus's miracles had nothing in common with the magic known to us in the third century, whereby the magicians tried to incite gods or spirits with incantations; Jesus simply spoke with the authority of God.[32]

The spoken commands of Jesus in John 4:50, 5:8, 9:7, and 11:43 do not ask for assistance but simply state a directive that comes to fruition. McPhee wrote that Greek mythology speaks of runners and chariots moving across the water at rapid speeds; however, these are unparalleled to Jesus, who did not run but walked on water.[33] The uniqueness of Jesus's walking on water is more a levitation miracle than superhuman speed on the water. While history may record isolated events whereby miracles occurred, these by no means invalidate the authentic content of the signs in John's gospel. History does not record the turning of water into wine without something inserted in the liquid, nor does it tell of the healing of a person from a command given in a city approximately fifteen miles away.

The feeding of the five thousand is sometimes compared to the feeding of the Israelites in the wilderness, and the manna came from heaven. In contrast, the fish and loaves of bread were multiplied by Jesus on earth to the extent that all the people were filled, and twelve baskets of leftovers were taken up. There are resurrection stories in history, but the uniqueness of Jesus's speaking life to a four-day-old dead corpus and resurrecting Lazarus is unique. We will examine each sign as to whether the immediate audience authenticates these.

---

[32] Keener, 259.

[33] Brian D. McPhee, "Walk, Don't Run: Jesus' Water Walking Is Unparalleled in Greco-Roman Mythology," *Journal of Biblical Literature* 135, no. 4 (2016): 763–777.

Similar Signs in the Synoptic and the Response

The feeding of the five thousand and Jesus's walking on water are two of John's signs recorded in the Synoptics. Borchert also comments that the two strategic signs of John 6 are parallel to those presented in the Synoptics.[34] Some theologians believe that the healing of the nobleman's son (4:46–54) is similar to the healing of the centurion's servant (Matt. 8:5–13; Luke 7:1–10). Brown suggests that the story of the healing of the nobleman's son is a third variant of the story of the centurion's boy in Matthew and Luke with minor details.[35] However, I would contend that there are too many major detailed differences between these passages to tie them together. Geographically, Matthew and Luke place Jesus entering Capernaum, while John's writing suggests the nobleman traveled from Capernaum to Cana to request Jesus come to Capernaum. Kostenberger reminds us that travel from Cana of Galilee to Capernaum was a day's journey of about fourteen miles.[36] In John's gospel, the requestor is a nobleman, while in Matthew, the requestor is a centurion, and in Luke, it is the elders and then the friends of the centurion. In Matthew and Luke, Jesus consents to go and heal the centurion's son, whereas, in John, Jesus does not go but speaks a word of healing. In Matthew and Luke, Jesus compliments the requestor, whereas He gives a rebuke in John. These are just a few of the differences but enough to conclude that the sign of the healing of the nobleman's son is significantly different from the centurion's servant's healing. Therefore, we will consider only the narratives of feeding the five thousand and Jesus' walking on water as parallels within the Synoptics.

---

[34] G. L. Borchert, *John 1–11* Vol. 25A. (Nashville: Broadman and Holman Publishers, 1996), 38.

[35] Raymond E. Brown, *The Gospel and Epistles of John: A Concise Commentary* (Collegeville, MI: Liturgical Press, 1988), 38–39.

[36] Kostenberger, 170.

The feeding of the five thousand is recorded in John 6:1–14 and Matthew 14:13–21, Mark 6:32–44, and Luke 9:10–17. John gives us the reaction of the men fed in verse fourteen: "Then those men, when they had seen the sign that Jesus did, said, 'This is truly the Prophet who is to come into the world.'" John also gives the reader insight into Jesus's knowledge of the multitude's desire to make Him a king (6:15). While the multitude does not express this desire to make Jesus a king, it still falls short of proclaiming the deity of Jesus Christ. After Jesus walks on water (6:52), Mark tells us later that the disciples did not understand the sign of the loaves. Matthew and Luke do not provide any audience reaction to the miracle of feeding the five thousand.

Moloney advocates that this miracle is a reminder of what Moses did for the children of Israel in the wilderness. The meal serves as a Eucharistic celebration with the breaking and distributing of bread, plus the gathering up of the fragments.[37] However, the scripture tells us only of loaves of bread and fish, while nothing is mentioned of wine or the symbolism of bread and wine. Furthermore, the scripture is silent on the audience's reaction if indeed this meal is symbolic of a Eucharistic celebration. John does not include any of Jesus's Lord's Supper remarks while feeding the five thousand. However, when instituting the Lord's Supper in Matthew 26:26–29, Mark 14:22–25, or Luke 22:17–20, Jesus speaks of His body, His blood, and the new covenant. Culpepper contends that Jesus fulfilled the role of the prophet described in Deuteronomy 18:13–18 when feeding the five thousand.[38] I would agree with Culpepper; however, the recognition of Jesus as the Prophet is short of realizing the deity of Jesus Christ. When we examine the passage of the feeding of the multitude, it is difficult to connect the dots and conclude that the immediate

---

[37] Francis J. Moloney, S. D. B. *The Gospel of John,* Sacra Pagina Series Vol.4. (Collegeville, MI: The Liturgical Press, 2005), 198.

[38] R. Alan Culpepper, *The Gospel and Letters of John* (Nashville: Abingdon Press, 1988), 153.

audience believed multiplying the loaves and fish equates to the deity of Jesus Christ.

Jesus's walking on water is in John 6:15–21, Matthew 14:22–33, and Mark 6:45–52. Matthew's gospel is the only writing that definitively gives the reaction of the disciples as "worshipping Him" and saying, "Truly You are the Son of God" (14:33). Mark alludes to the disciples' lack of faith, and John does not indicate that the disciples believe in the deity of Jesus Christ. Culpepper suggests that "the statement 'It is I' (Greek *"ego eimi"*) can mean 'I am,' divine self-disclosure of His being the incarnate Logos and one greater than Moses."[39] However, there is nothing in John's passage to suggest that these disciples understood the words of Jesus in relationship to deity. John only tells us that they received Him into the boat, which is short of definitive proof of His deity.

The fact that John's writing does not include Matthew's reaction in terms of worshipping Jesus raises several questions in the area of source criticism: (1) If John's writing is dependent on Matthew. It would make sense for him to include the disciples' reaction to solidify the deity of Jesus's walking on water. (2) If John's writing is the result of redaction within the Johannine community, then the redactors missed an opportunity to blatantly support the deity of Jesus Christ by elaborating on the reaction of the disciples. Kostenberger contends that when Jesus walked on water, it was a private demonstration of His messianic glory to the disciples only and did not warrant being considered a Johannine sign.[40]

Personal manifestations of signs do not warrant exclusion, especially considering that the turning of water to wine occurred at a wedding where only a few people knew Jesus had performed this miracle. Furthermore, this water-walking sign that appears in three of the four Gospels adds validity to its being a Johannine sign. Dunnett views this sign as confirmation of Jesus's power over natural

---

[39] Ibid., 157.

[40] Kostenberger, 205.

laws.[41] Michaels's position is that walking on water and calming the storm are not the actual miracles; rather, Jesus's crossing the sea is about the Spirit blowing where it wills.[42] Jesus's walking on water is debatable as a sign of His deity, but collectively, this sign collaborates with the Johannine group for the readers during the early and later church.

Our study will include an examination of the traditional seven signs within the gospel of John with a focus on the uniqueness of the signs and their impact upon the audience. We will address the seven traditional signs: Jesus turning water to wine, His healing the nobleman's son, Jesus healing the man at the pool of Bethesda, Jesus feeding the five thousand, Jesus' walking on water, Jesus healing the man born blind, and Jesus raising Lazarus from the dead. We will also address two debatable signs: Jesus cleansing the temple in John 2 and the large catch of fish in John 21. Last, we will discuss the ultimate sign, the resurrection of Jesus Christ, and the final conclusions of our study.

The following is an outline summary of the sign passages and subject material to be examined within the gospel of John, beginning with chapter 3.

I. **Chapter 3: Jesus Turns Water to Wine**
    A. Background information: Cana, Jewish weddings
    B. Characters involved in the miracle: Mary, Jesus, servants, governor, disciples
    C. Explanation of the miraculous event: requestor, obedience, power of the word, recognition of wine
    D. Other miracles similar to the transformation of water
    E. Impact of the miracle on attending audience

---

41 W. M. Dunnett, *Exploring the New Testament* (Wheaton, IL: Crossway Books, 2001), 24–25.

42 Michaels, *The Gospel of John*, 358.

    F. Impact of the miracle on the church (early and present-day)

    G. Whether this sign gives sufficient reason to believe Jesus is the Son of God

II. Chapter 4: Jesus Heals the Nobleman's Son

    A. Background information: Cana, Capernaum

    B. Characters involved in the miracle: nobleman, Jesus, nobleman's son, servants, and household

    C. Explanation of the miraculous event: dialogue with the requestor and the audience, power of the spoken word, faith in action

    D. Other miracles similar to the healing of the nobleman's son: uniqueness of this sign

    E. Impact of the miracle on the nobleman, his son, and the family/household

    F. Impact of the miracle on the church (early and present-day)

    G. Whether this sign gives sufficient reason to believe Jesus is the Son of God

III. Chapter 5: Jesus Heals the Man at the Pool of Bethesda

    A. Background information: Jerusalem, sheep gate, Bethesda, porches

    B. Characters involved in the scene: the multitude of people, theory of angel stirring the water, a man sick for thirty-eight years, Jesus, Jews

    C. Explanation of the miracle: Jesus initiates contact with the man, dialogue with the man, power of Jesus to heal

    D. Impact of the miracle on the man and the Jews

    E. Other miracles similar to the healing of the man at the pool: uniqueness of this sign

    F. Impact of the miracle on the church (early and present-day)

    G. Whether this sign gives sufficient reason to believe Jesus is the Son of God

IV. **Chapter 6: Jesus Feeds the Five Thousand**

    A. Background information: Sea of Galilee, mountainside, the feast of the Jews, Passover

    B. Characters involved in the miracle: Jesus, the multitude, disciples, Philip and Andrew, the lad

    C. Explanation of the miracle: Jesus tests the disciples' faith, blessing and breaking, overabundance, fragments

    D. Other miracles similar to the feeding of the five thousand: Moses in the wilderness, Elisha feeding, Synoptic narratives of feeding

    E. Impact of the miracle on the audience: plenty of food, prophet, king

    F. Impact of the miracle on the church (early and present-day)

    G. Whether this sign gives sufficient reason to believe Jesus is the Son of God

V. **Chapter 7: Jesus Walks on Water**

    A. Background information: Sea of Tiberias, historical weather conditions

    B. Characters involved in the miracle: Jesus, disciples

    C. Explanation of the miracle: power over natural laws

    D. Other miracles similar to Jesus walking on water

    E. Impact of the miracle on the disciples

    F. Impact of the miracle on the church (early and present-day)

    G. Whether this sign gives sufficient reason to believe Jesus is the Son of God

VI. Chapter 8: Jesus Heals the Man Born Blind

A. Background information: the temple in Jerusalem
B. Characters involved: the man born blind, parents of the man born blind, Jesus, disciples of Jesus, neighbors of the man born blind, Pharisees
C. Explanation of the miracle: sin versus the glory of God, Jesus performs the miracle
D. Other miracles similar to Jesus healing the man born blind
E. Impact of the miracle on the attending audience
F. Impact of the miracle on the church (early and present-day)
G. Whether this sign gives sufficient reason to believe Jesus is the Son of God

VII. Chapter 9: Jesus Raises Lazarus from the Grave

A. Background information: Bethany near Jerusalem
B. Characters involved: Jesus, Lazarus, Mary, Martha, disciples, Jews
C. Dialogue: prior to Bethany with disciples, misunderstanding of sleep and resurrection, Mary and Martha at Bethany
D. Explanation of the miracle: status of Lazarus's body/ time factor, Jesus wept, the stone, the prayer, the declaration by Jesus, Lazarus resurrected, grave clothes
E. Other miracles similar to Jesus resurrecting Lazarus
F. Impact of the miracle on the attending audience
G. Impact of the miracle on the church (early and present-day).
H. Whether this sign gives sufficient reason to believe Jesus is the Son of God

VIII. Chapter 10: Debatable Signs
  A. Jesus cleansing the temple
  B. The large catch of fish

IX. Chapter 11: The Ultimate Sign—The Resurrection of Jesus Christ
  A. The empty tomb
  B. Witnesses to the empty tomb
  C. Witnesses to the resurrected Jesus
      1. Mary Magdalene as a witness
      2. The disciples as witnesses
      3. The disciples' second witness of the resurrected Jesus
      4. Other witnesses to the resurrected Jesus

X. Chapter 12: Final Conclusions

Final assumptions and conclusions of our study should clarify whether there is sufficient evidence for the immediate audience, the early church, and the present-day church to believe John's signs provide proof of the deity of Jesus Christ.

CHAPTER 3

Jesus Turns Water to Wine

Background Information

Jesus turning water into wine was performed in the small town of Cana of Galilee. Two ancient sites are probable locations for John's Cana of Galilee: "Kefr Kenna, which is about four miles northeast of Nazareth, and Khirbet Kana (also spelled Qana or Cana), which is further north, about nine miles from Nazareth."[43]

Contemporary scholarship, however, has almost unanimously settled on Khirbet Kana as the site of NT Cana. Archaeologists exploring at the site have found pottery from the Hebrew monarchy period (*c.* BC 900–600), as well as from Hellenistic, Roman, Arabic, and Crusader times.[44]

---

[43] J. E. Miller, "Cana of Galilee," *The Lexham Bible Dictionary,* eds. J. D. Barry, D. Bomar, D. R. Brown, R. Klippenstein, D. Mangum, C. Sinclair Wolcott, … W. Widder, (Bellingham, WA: Lexham Press, 2016).

[44] W. A. Elwell and B. J. Beitzel, "Cana," *Baker Encyclopedia of the Bible*, Vol. 1 (Grand Rapids, MI: Baker Book House, 1988), 406.

John's gospel informs us that this Cana of Galilee was the location of the healing of the nobleman's son (4:46) as well as the hometown of Nathanael, a disciple of Jesus (21:2). This study of John will assume the town of Khirbet Kana to be the location of the first miracle, especially when considering the fact that "modern Khirbet Kana is closely adjacent to an area where reeds still grow, relating to the root meaning of 'Cana.'"[45]

First-century Jewish marriages began with a betrothal period, and during this time, the man and woman were referred to as husband and wife even though they did not live together. Edersheim states that "at the betrothal, the bridegroom, personally or by deputy, handed to the bride a piece of money or a letter, it being expressly stated in each case that the man thereby espoused the woman. A legal document (the *Shitré Erusin*) fixed the dowry which each brought, the mutual obligations, and all other legal points."[46] The actual wedding ceremony included a "procession to the bride's home led by the groom, who then escorted her back to their new residence,"[47] followed by a wedding feast that could last a week or even longer. A Jewish betrothal and the subsequent wedding activities were far more extensive in terms of preparation, celebration, and commitment than the normal engagement and weddings of Western civilization today. Let us now consider the characters involved in this miracle at Cana of Galilee.

Characters Involved

Jesus's mother is not named in John's gospel, and perhaps Carson is correct in stating that this was done to avoid confusion with the

---

[45] Miller, "Cana of Galilee," *The Lexham Bible Dictionary.*

[46] Edersheim, *The Life and Times of Jesus the Messiah,* 353–354.

[47] J. S. Deere, "Song of Songs," *The Bible Knowledge Commentary: An Exposition of the Scriptures,* vol. 1, eds. J. F. Walvoord and R. B. Zuck, (Wheaton, IL: Victor Books, 1985), 1016.

other women named Mary in the gospel.[48] Even in John 19:25, she is referred to as the mother of Jesus without specifically naming her. Michaels suggests that Jesus's "mother's presence provides a reason for the presence of Jesus and His disciples"[49]; however, I agree with Carson that Jesus, His mother, and His disciples were invited to the wedding of a relative or close friend of the family.[50] Mary's statement to Jesus that "they have no wine" indicates that Mary had some role of responsibility in the wedding activities. Her interactive request to Jesus should not spiritually or theologically elevate her to an intermediary position between people and Jesus.[51] I would again agree with Carson that the mother of Jesus is similar to others within the gospel writings who interacted with Jesus by making requests of Him. There is no indication from the narrative story that the mother of Jesus anticipated Jesus's performing a miracle, and John tells us in 2:11 that this was the "beginning of signs Jesus did in Cana of Galilee." The mother of Jesus, whom the Synoptic writers call Mary, is simply a mother requesting her son to avoid the social embarrassment of not having a sufficient amount of wine.

John's gospel does not name or give the number of disciples attending the wedding with Jesus. However, we can speculate based on John 1:35–51 that there were probably four, maybe five, disciples (Andrew, Peter, Philip, Nathanael, and an unnamed disciple) with Jesus at the wedding. The unnamed disciple in 1:35 could be the beloved disciple mentioned in 21:20 and 24. The group of disciples has no function at the wedding except merely to serve as witnesses to the miracle of Jesus turning water to wine and to believe in Him (2:11).

The number of servants and their names are excluded as this information is not critical to the miracle story. The servants are

---

[48] Carson, 168.
[49] Michaels, 141.
[50] Carson, 169.
[51] Ibid.

spiritually noteworthy because of their willingness to be obedient to
the instructions of Jesus, after being told by Mary, "Whatever he says
to you, do it" (2:5). The servants are also witnesses to the miracle of
Jesus turning water into wine (2:9); however, John does not tell us
whether these servants believed in Jesus.

The master of the feast, "to whom the servants bring the wine,
is probably a chief steward or head waiter, in charge of catering and
perhaps of the place where the banquet was held."[52] The master of
the feast is a part of the miracle verification process even though he
does not know where the wine came from or how (2:9). Knowles
states, "When the master of the banquet tastes the water, he discovers
an excellent wine. This is a miracle of new creation."[53] He addresses
the bridegroom because the bridegroom is responsible for providing
all the food and drink for the wedding celebration.[54] The statement
by the master of the feast to the bridegroom in 2:9 suggests the
wine Jesus made is of superior quality compared with the previous
wine. We will discuss the components of the wine and the various
theories concerning the wine of that period in the next section of the
explanation of the miracle.

The bridegroom is not named, nor do we hear anything about
him until the statement made to him by the master of the feast (2:10).
We cannot help but think of the spiritual symbolism that portrays
Jesus as the church's bridegroom and His role in offering the "good
wine." Elowsky contends that the wedding is symbolic of the Word
(Jesus as the bridegroom) coming from heaven to earth and offering
His bride the spiritual seeds of wisdom and an invitation to His
home.[55] The face value of the text (2:10) does not provide a response

---

[52] Carson, 174.

[53] A. Knowles, *The Bible Guide*, 1st Augsburg books ed. (Minneapolis: Augsburg,
2001), 509.

[54] Carson, 174.

[55] Joel C. Elowsky, *Ancient Christian Commentary on Scripture*, New Testament
IVa John 1–10 (Downers Grove, IL: InterVarsity Press, 2006), 89.

from the bridegroom regarding the statement from the master of the feast, so we will not speculate at this time.

Jesus is justifiably the primary character in this sign narrative. The initial request is made to Him by His mother, the servants are willing to follow His instructions, the master of the feast verifies the quality of the wine, and ultimately the disciples believe in Him. I do not believe it is by coincidence that John's gospel tells us of Jesus, who is described as the Eternal Word or Logos (1:1–4), being invited to the wedding celebration, which the Lord instituted in the Garden of Eden (Genesis 2:24). John 2:2 tells us that Jesus and His disciples were invited to the wedding instead of just showing up or, in our present language, crashing the wedding. There are numerous overtones to Jesus's being invited to the wedding, one of which is the implication that modern traditional wedding ceremonies can use as a foundation of the fact that Jesus approved of the marriage institution.[56] Jesus, as the Creator and sustainer of life (1:1–4), attends this wedding celebration and performs the first sign pointing to His supernatural identity. We will inject more comments about Jesus as we explain the miraculous event of turning water into wine.

Explanation of the Miraculous Event

Jesus's mother directs her request, "They have no wine," toward Jesus in anticipation of a forthcoming solution. The expected solution is evidenced in verse five, when she says to the servants, "Whatever He says to you, do it." I believe it is an unlikely conclusion to suggest that Mary expected a miracle because John tells us this is the beginning of miracles in Jesus's ministry. It is more likely to believe that Mary had grown to depend on Jesus for the family's financial support and problem-solving, especially since Joseph, her husband, is not mentioned. What Mary expects of Jesus is merely a resolution

---

[56] Carson, 168.

to the shortage of wine, and she exercises faith by instructing the servants to be obedient to Jesus's instructions. Edersheim supports this position when he writes,

> And so when she told Him of the want that had arisen, it was simply in absolute confidence in her Son, probably without any conscious expectancy of a miracle on His part. Yet not without a touch of maternal self-consciousness, almost pride, that He, Whom she could trust to do anything that was needed, was her Son, Whom she could solicit in the friendly family whose guests they were—and if not for her sake, yet at her request.[57]

Mary's request to Jesus should not be blown out of spiritual proportion to suggest elevating her to a higher religiously or theologically status. Borchert advocates that "writers on Mariology who have argued that Mary's so-called persistence resulted in Jesus' subsequent action"[58] are unjustified when considering Jesus's commitment to do the Father's will as opposed to satisfying human interests. Jesus was never coerced into doing anything, as evidenced in John 7:3–8 and 11:3–6. John consistently makes the case in his gospel that Jesus's mission was to do the Father's will. Neyrey also supports this position that Jesus honored the Father: He wanted to do "His Father's will (4:34; 5:30; 6:38–40; 12:43) and seek only the Father's glory (7:18; 8:49–50). In this respect, Jesus models the ideal response of a client to a patron quite differently from many in his audience, who seek their own glory."[59] Therefore, I believe it was not Mary's relationship to Jesus that prompted the turning of water into

---

[57] Edersheim, *The Life and Times of Jesus the Messiah*, 360–361.

[58] Borchert, 156.

[59] Jerome Neyrey, *The Gospel of John* (New York: Cambridge University Press, 2007), 23.

wine but Jesus's obedience to the Father's will to inspire faith in the One sent by the Father.

Jesus's response to Mary's request seems abrupt and harsh, considering this is His earthly mother. Carson states, "The form of address, *gynai* (New International Version, or NIV, 'Dear woman') though thoroughly courteous is not normally an endearing term, nor the form of address preferred by a son addressing a much-loved mother."[60] Jesus's response appears to distance Him from His mother and set the priority of His earthly mission. Brown states that John uses "the term woman here to show rejection by Jesus from a human sphere of action but reserving a much richer role at the cross."[61] Jesus's words, "What does your concern have to do with Me? My hour has not yet come" (2:4) would imply an act of disengagement from His mother and the wedding activities. Michaels agrees that Jesus's words are a possible disengagement from both His mother and the wedding banquet.[62] I tend to believe that Jesus, knowing in advance what He would do as in John 7:2–10 and 11:1–7, distances Himself from earthly cares and sets the priority of the hour, which we know is the cross of Jesus Christ.

Mary's instructions to the servants (2:5) and their obedience set the stage for the miracle of Jesus turning water into wine. A few comments regarding the water pots are in order. The six waterpots of stone used in accordance with Jewish purification protocols (2:6) have been theorized by numerous scholars. Carson tells us that stoneware, as opposed to earthenware, is more conducive to cleanliness, making it more suitable for ceremonial washing.[63] The number 6 concerning the waterpots could suggest the incompleteness of the present Jewish ceremonial system until the new covenant by

---

[60] Carson, 170.

[61] Brown, *The Gospels and the Epistles of John*, 28–29.

[62] Michaels, 144.

[63] Carson, 173.

Jesus Christ.[64] The amount of water in the waterpots (2:6) suggests an excessive amount of water for purification. Edersheim comments that the excessive amount of water was used for Jewish purification of hands before and after eating, plus the cleaning of vessels utilized in meal preparation.[65]

It is these six waterpots that Jesus instructs the servants to fill with water, and they obey His instructions to the extent of filling them to the top. John does not give us any reason to believe that these servants complained or murmured at the instructions of Jesus; they simply obeyed. We do not know how long it took to fill these six waterpots (possibly 120 to 180 gallons based upon 2:6) or by what means they could transport water from wherever the source was located nearby. We know they were obedient to the commands of Jesus's mother and the instructions of Jesus.

There is much symbolism and speculation regarding the filling of the water pots. According to Edersheim, the significant action of filling the water pots to the brim could perhaps eliminate the possibility of something other than water being added.[66] Keener says that the filling is symbolic of other scriptural passages whereby people were filled with food (6:11–12) or filled with joy (3:29; 15:11; 16:24; 17:13) or even the Word, who is filled with grace and truth (1:14, 16).[67] I also see symbolism in terms of being filled with the Spirit as expressed in 3:24, the implication being that these six waterpots were filled in such a fashion that nothing else could be added to them: "And they filled them up to the brim" (2:7).

Afterward, Jesus exerts the power of the spoken word. He instructs the servants to "draw some out now, and take it to the master of the feast" (2:8). We do not know precisely when the water was turned to wine, but we do know that six waterpots that once

---

[64] Ibid., 174.

[65] Edersheim, *The Life and Times of Jesus the Messiah*, 357.

[66] Edersheim, *The Life and Times of Jesus the Messiah*, 362.

[67] Keener, 513.

were used for purification have now been transformed into six wine pots for drinking. "At this point, the miracle is already accomplished, but no one except Jesus knows it."[68] Jesus has not only turned water into wine, but He has provided an overabundance of wine for the remainder of the wedding feast.[69] Jesus uses the word *draw* (*antleo*), which is commonly used for drawing water from a well, except now the source cannot be a resource from a water supply but rather a well of wine from the Creator Himself. Torrey advocates that "by turning the water into a wholesome wine, He showed His creative power and manifested His glory."[70] John's writing of this miracle connects Jesus with the prologue statement, "All things were made through Him, and without Him, nothing was made that was made" (1:3).

We cannot help but recall other instances in scripture where the divine spoken word brought about manifested change. In Genesis 1, when God spoke, things appeared in the creation of heaven and earth, and John tells us in 1:1, "The Word was with God and the Word was God." The Word or the Logos who initiated the creation of all things was now at a wedding demonstrating the spoken word of turning water to wine. I would surmise that even though Jesus did not audibly speak directly to the water, the intent of His words to the servants agreed with His divine purpose of changing the water to wine. We will now consider the recognition and quality of the wine.

The master of the feast is the primary character concerning the recognition of the wine and its quality. After tasting the wine, he notices that its quality is superior to that of the wine previously served and comments to the bridegroom in 2:10, "Every man at the beginning sets out the good wine, and when the guests have well drunk, then the inferior. You have kept the good wine until now!" There has been much written about whether this wine created by

---

[68] Michaels, 151.

[69] Keener, 513.

[70] R. A. Torrey, *Difficulties in the Bible: Alleged Errors and Contradictions* (Willow Grove, PA: Woodlawn Electronic Publishing, 1998), 147.

Jesus was an intoxicating drink and how it compares to today's wine. Perhaps we should make some brief comments about historical aspects of wine during the New Testament period.

Ainslie informs us that "there were three kinds of wine in Palestine—the fermented, which was used by dilution, the unfermented, and the boiled juice of the grape, which usually stopped fermentation."[71] Today's wine, by biblical standards, would be considered a strong drink because unmixed wine was not the norm. Geisler states,

> What the Bible frequently meant by wine was basically purified water. Stein researched wine-drinking in the ancient world, in Jewish sources, and in the Bible. He pointed out that wine in Homer's day was twenty parts water and one part wine (Odyssey 9.208–9). Pliny referred to wine as eight parts water and one part wine (Natural History 14.6.54). According to Aristophanes, it was stronger: three parts water and two parts wine. Other classical Greek writers spoke of other mixtures: Euenos—three parts water, one part wine; Hesiod—three to one, water to wine; Alexis—four to one; Diodes and Anacreon—two to one; and Ion—three to one. The average was about three or four parts of water to one part of wine.[72]

The mixture of wine seemed to be a common practice in the New Testament period; however, there is no indication of a mixture involved in this miracle. The quality of wine appeared to be the ultimate responsibility of the bridegroom, as stated in 2:10. Geisler

---

[71] P. Ainslie, "Among the Gospels and the Acts being Notes and Comments Covering the Life of Christ in the Flesh, and the First Thirty Years' History of His Church" (Baltimore: Temple Seminary Press, 1908): 234–235.

[72] Norman L. Geisler, "The Bible Does Not Teach that New Testament Communion Wine was Unfermented," *Bibliotheca sacra* 139, no. 553 (January–March 1982): 46–56.

also suggests that "according to the Talmud the 'wine' used in the Passover meal was three parts water and one part wine (cf. 2 Macc. 15:39). It may also be that the wine Jesus miraculously provided at the wedding in Cana (John 2:1–11) was a similar drink, that is, wine mixed with water."[73]

We will never know the ratio of wine to water at the wedding in Cana, but we do know that the six waterpots were filled with water to the brim and miraculously turned to wine. Torrey, however, does not believe Jesus made an intoxicating drink because new wine must go through the process of decay, and in the case of the wedding at Cana, fermentation had not occurred. In essence, Torrey is suggesting that the new wine was grape juice.[74] I believe Torrey is trying to apply the rules of nature in terms of wine's aging to a miraculous event whereby water is turned into wine. Geisler wrote, "In John 2:9–10 it is called 'wine' (οἶνος) and 'good wine' (καλόν οἰνον). These are the same words used for fermented wine elsewhere in the New Testament (cf. Mark 2:22; Eph. 5:18)."[75]

Gangel advocates that it is unimaginable "that people who had been drinking throughout the evening would not immediately recognize a switch from normal wine to grape juice."[76] I agree with Gangel and conclude from the master of the feast statement (2:10) that the new wine was superior to the previous wine. Regarding the miracle of turning water into wine, whether it is fermented or nonfermented does not matter. Jesus turning water into wine is only an issue for those who are strict in the absence of wine. Foster states, "It is useless to debate about what kind of wine this was. The making of it was a miracle; therefore, the product was unique. The taste was

---

[73] Ibid.

[74] Torrey, 147.

[75] Geisler, 46–56.

[76] K. O. Gangel, *John* Vol. 4 (Nashville: Broadman and Holman Publishers, 2000), 31.

better than any they had had before."[77] Let us now consider whether there are similar miracles involving the transformation of water.

Other Miracles Similar to the Transformation of Water

Jesus's turning water into wine has been unique throughout history. First, the transformation of water in the miracle of Moses turning water into blood in Exodus 7:14–24 does not compare. Moses's miracle was a sign of the judgment of God, whereas the miracle of Jesus was a sign of the joy He will give through the Holy Spirit.[78] It appears in Exodus 7:22 that the magicians of Egypt were able to transform some small quantity of water into blood; however, they were unable to reverse the miracle of Moses, and therefore Pharaoh did not believe in God.[79] Second, the mythological Dionysus tradition of a river of wine on an unknown island is believed to have resulted from many large grapevines, full of clusters, which gave rise to a river.[80] However, this is not an example of a transformation of water to wine as at the wedding at Cana and, therefore, cannot be considered a comparable miracle. At best, this river of wine was due to an overabundance of grapes producing a river and not the result of any transformation of water to wine.

The uniqueness of Jesus's turning water into wine is further highlighted by the new wine's quality being superior to the old wine. So, I contend that there is a lack of comparable examples of individuals performing a miracle of turning water into wine. Let's now look at the impact of this miracle on the attending audience.

---

[77] L. Foster, *John: Unlocking the Scriptures for You* (Cincinnati: Standard, 1987), 33.

[78] E. A. Blum, "John," in *The Bible Knowledge Commentary: An Exposition of the Scriptures,* Vol. 2, eds. J. F. Walvoord and R. B. Zuck, (Wheaton, IL: Victor Books, 1985), 278–279.

[79] H. D. M. Spence-Jones, "Exodus," *The Pulpit Commentary* Vol. 1 (Peabody, MA: Hendrickson, 1909), 176–177.

[80] Elowsky, 249.

Impact of This Miracle on the Attending Audience

Several characters recognized the miracle of Jesus's turning water into wine. I would view the servants as silent witnesses since they exercised faith to follow the directive of Mary and the instructions of Jesus to fill the water pots and then draw some out for the master of the feast. They undoubtedly realized that they put water in the pots, and somehow the water became wine when tasted by the master of the feast. John does not address the servants' reaction; he only informs the reader that the servants knew where the wine had come from (2:9). Keener agrees with us that John writes about the servants to add validity regarding the actual miracle performed. It is also conceivable that John contrasts the knowledge of the servants of lower social status to that of the guests of a higher social status.[81] The servants know where the wine came from, but the master of the feast does not know.

The disciples of Jesus are also silent witnesses in that John tells us only that they believed in Him (2:11). Based upon John's testimony, we must contend that the disciples observed the instructions of Jesus to the servants, their obedience, and the testimony of the master of the feast.

Jesus's mother, the master of the feast, and the bridegroom are all characters identified at the wedding, but John does not tell us of their knowledge of water turning to wine. Michaels comments on the irony of the banquet master verifying the miracle while not realizing he is even verifying a miracle.[82] The humorous remark to the bridegroom is evidence of his lack of knowledge of how the wine came about. John's closing remarks in this narrative are silent regarding Jesus's mother and brothers (possibly attending the wedding) having knowledge of the miracle and belief in Jesus. Only the disciples believe (2:11–12), which we can call sign-faith.

---

[81] Keener, 514–515.
[82] Michaels, 151.

The revelation of Jesus's glory is expressed in 2:11; however, John does not tell us who recognized the glory of Jesus, though we could speculate that it was the disciples. While the manifested glory of Jesus is a common expression related to Isaiah 40:5 and in the prologue (1:14), we cannot help but think of this miracle as a foretaste of the future glory of His cross and exaltation. Let us now consider the impact of this miracle on the church.

Impact of this Miracle on the Church (early and present-day)

The impact of Jesus's turning water into wine in such an abundant quantity could cause the early church to reflect on Jewish precepts from the Old Testament history while prompting some Christians who converted from Hellenism to recall stories of Dionysos, the Greek god of wine. Readers of the Old Testament will recall that Isaiah (25:6–9), Amos (9:13), and Joel (3:18) all prophesied a period in Jewish history that God would supernaturally intervene and cause an abundance of wine. Edwards tells us that "*2 Baruch* 29 foretells that when the 'Anointed One' (messiah) begins to be revealed vines will produce supernaturally large quantities of grapes. Targums and rabbinic sources associate abundance of fine wine with the messianic age (Aus, 1988, pp. 8f)."[83] While the method in which wine was generated differs from Jesus's turning water into wine and wine as a product of large quantities of grapes, the sign or miracle performed by Jesus would direct us toward the messianic age.

Christians influenced by a Hellenistic background might see some similarities to the stories of the legendary Dionysos, whose ship turned into a grape-laden vine, which caused his ship to have a sweet

---

[83] Edwards, *Discovering John* (London: Society for Promoting Christian Knowledge, 2003), 51.

wine fragrance.[84] While this is not the transformation of water to wine, Edwards also states that "according to Pausanias (VI.26.1f.), on the eve of Dionysos' feast empty jars placed in his temple at Elis were miraculously filled overnight with wine. At his festival on Andros and Teos, the temple springs miraculously flowed with wine instead of water (Pliny, *NH*, II.231, XXXI.16; Diod. Sic., III.66.2)."[85] I must add that the stories of Dionysos are pure mythology without any outstanding support or true comparison to the miracle of Jesus's turning water into wine without utilizing grapes.

The impact of the miracle is best read in the testimony of John 2:11: "And His disciples believed in Him." Lenski states, "They rested their confidence in him as the Messiah and did this in consequence of the sign here wrought. Following their original acceptance and faith, as recounted in the previous chapter, ἐπίστευσαν here implies an increase of faith."[86] There is a distinction between the servants and the disciples in realizing a miracle and having faith in Jesus. The servants knew a miracle had occurred, but the disciples believed in Him because of the miracle and saw His glory.[87] The disciples who became the apostles of the early church testified of the impact of this miracle through their following of Jesus and commitment to being witnesses of Him (Acts 4:19–20).

The later church would view the miracle in terms of what it signified instead of the product produced. McGarvey and Pendleton state that the miracle "manifested the glory of Christ, part of which glory is his power to change the worse into the better, the simpler into the richer. It is the glory of Christ that he can transform sinners

---

[84] Ibid., 52.

[85] Ibid.

[86] R. C. H. Lenski, *The Interpretation of St. John's Gospel* (Minneapolis: Augsburg Publishing House, 1961), 200.

[87] Carson, 175.

into his own likeness (1 John 3:2; 1 Cor. 15:42–44; Phil. 3:20–21)."[88] The later church reads of this miracle of turning water to wine and must decide to believe or not to believe and then draw speculations on the symbolism of the quality and quantity of wine. The miracle illustrates Jesus as the solution to life's daily problems in that He can create life and provide joy in crises.

Whether This Sign Gives Sufficient Reason to Believe Jesus Is the Son of God

I believe this sign gives sufficient reason to believe Jesus is the Son of God for two reasons:

1) The uniqueness of turning water to wine can only be documented as being performed by Jesus. The Old Testament account of Moses turning water to blood is an act of judgment instead of providing life and joy. The mythology of Dionysus includes the elements of grapes, whereas Jesus uses only His creative power. Verifying the quality and quantity clearly indicates the superiority of the wine to the previous wine and an amount more than sufficient for the wedding at Cana. No other miracles in history can compare with this sign of who Jesus is.

2) The impact of the miracle in terms of belief by the disciples and revealed glory is definitively a testimony of the identity of Jesus. Keener agrees that the disciples believed based upon the sign; however, the sign-faith is not the highest form of discipleship.[89] Lenski contends

---

[88] J. W. McGarvey, and P. Y. Pendleton, *The Four-Fold Gospel* (Cincinnati: The Standard Publishing Company, 1914), 118–119.

[89] Keener, 516.

that signs always require faith in what is signified, coupled with obedience on the part of those who see the signs. The term as well as its sense were well known to the Jews from the Old Testament, were constantly used in the apostolic church, and, doubtless, were used by Jesus himself to designate his own works. John's Gospel naturally uses this term in the sense of the strongest and the most tangible testimony for Jesus' divinity, always counting those guilty who meet the signs with unbelief.[90]

John's purpose in writing this miracle is tied to the prologue (1:14) and the purpose given in 20:31. We now turn our attention to the second sign in Cana of Galilee—Jesus's healing of the nobleman's son.

---

[90] Lenski, 199.

CHAPTER 4

Jesus Heals the Nobleman's Son

Background Information

Jesus returns to Cana of Galilee in John 4:46–54, where He performed the first miracle of turning water into wine. Laney informs us that "Douglas Edwards, in association with the University of Puget Sound, conducted excavations at Khirbet Kana in 1998–1999. He discovered Hellenistic and Roman houses and a large complex with monumental columns, apparently a Byzantine synagogue or church."[91] Based upon archaeological studies, this site of Cana of Galilee is probably at Khirbet Kana, nine miles north of Nazareth along the north edge of the Bet Netofa Valley, as opposed to the traditional Cana, which is located four miles northeast of Nazareth at Kefr Kenna.[92]

---

[91] J. C. Laney, "Galilee," in *The Lexham Bible Dictionary,* eds. J. D. Barry, D. Bomar, D. R. Brown, R. Klippenstein, D. Mangum, C. Sinclair Wolcott, … W. Widder, (Bellingham, WA: Lexham Press, 2016).

[92] Ibid.

Capernaum, however, is located "on the northwest shore of the Sea of Galilee about two and one-half miles west of the entrance of the Jordan," which is further north of Cana of Galilee.[93] Capernaum was a commerce center of fishing and trade, a Roman tax polling station of which Matthew was reportedly called as a disciple of Jesus (Matt. 9:9–10), and the home of Peter and his mother-in-law (Matt. 8:14).[94] Kostenberger tells us that Capernaum in proximity to Cana of Galilee was about fourteen miles or the equivalent of a day's journey, plus the trip was mostly uphill due to its being located in the Galilean hill country.[95] Let us now look at the characters involved in John's second miracle in Cana of Galilee, where Jesus heals the nobleman's son.

Characters Involved

There are characters referenced in the narrative, such as the nobleman's son and "you people" (4:48, probably regarding the Galilee audience), who do not have a speaking role but are listeners of the conversation of Jesus. The servants of the nobleman who have a speaking role are limited to informing the nobleman of the healing of his son and the time of healing (4:50–51). John does not identify the members of the nobleman's household (4:53) but merely ties this verse to his purpose in writing the gospel in 20:31. We can only speculate based on 4:53 that, since the nobleman's son would be a member of the household, he also believed in Jesus. There is no

---

[93] G. W. Knight, "Capernaum," in *Holman Illustrated Bible Dictionary*, eds. C. Brand, C. Draper, A. England, S. Bond, E. R. Clendenen, and T. C. Butler, (Nashville: Holman Bible Publishers, 2003), 263–265.

[94] M. B. Winstead, "Capernaum," in *The Lexham Bible Dictionary*, eds. J. D. Barry, D. Bomar, D. R. Brown, R. Klippenstein, D. Mangum, C. Sinclair Wolcott, ... W. Widder, (Bellingham, WA: Lexham Press, 2016).

[95] Kostenberger, 170.

further mention made of "you people" in 4:48, so we will be silent regarding their response to the words of Jesus.

The nobleman lived in Capernaum and had traveled to Cana of Galilee seeking Jesus after hearing of His coming to Galilee. Edersheim identifies the nobleman as possibly an officer of Herod Antipas, whose son was sick and at the point of death.[96] Foster gives insight on the meaning of *royal official* or *nobleman* as used in the New King James translation:

> The Greek word means literally "one pertaining to the king." Herod Antipas was king of Galilee, and this official probably was attached to his court or his army. (Some later followers of Jesus may have been influenced by this man: Joanna, whose husband was the manager of Herod's household, and Manaen, foster brother of Herod the tetrarch).[97]

Easton describes the nobleman as "an officer of state (John 4:49) in the service of Herod Antipas. He is supposed to have been the Chuza, Herod's steward, whose wife was one of those women who 'ministered unto the Lord of their substance'"[98] (Luke 8:3). Frankly, we do not have definitive knowledge of the nobleman's government position, nor can we declare that he was a Jew versus a Gentile. We know that this man "was clearly at his wit's end and desperately needed the help of the Saviour. He 'kept beseeching Him' to travel to Capernaum to heal his son."[99]

Jesus is the primary character in this narrative of the healing of the nobleman's son, and rightly so. The verses before 4:46 imply that Jesus is an itinerant preacher and teacher traveling from Judea

---

[96] Edersheim, *The Life and Times of Jesus the Messiah,* 424.

[97] Foster, 56.

[98] M. G. Easton, "Nobleman," *Easton's Bible Dictionary* (New York: Harper and Brothers, 1893).

[99] W.W. Wiersbe, *The Bible Exposition Commentary,* Vol. 1 (Wheaton, IL: Victor Books, 1996), 302–303.

to Galilee. Following the chronology of John 4, we must believe that Jesus has left Samaria after spending two days in their city (4:40, 43). He is now confronted by this nobleman (possibly a Gentile, as was the Samarian woman) needing His help. The welcome and reception that Jesus received from the Samarians (4:39–42) and the Galileans (4:45) directly contrast with that received in Judea. At this point, John has not specifically mentioned any miracles in Jerusalem unless we support the opinion of Kostenberger that the cleansing of the temple was the second sign of Jesus (2:13–25).[100] John does inform us that the Galileans "received Him, having seen all the things He did in Jerusalem at the feast; for they also had gone to the feast (4:45)." Verse 45 collaborates nicely with 20:30: "And truly Jesus did many other signs in the presence of His disciples, which are not written in this book." Let us now look at the miraculous event of Jesus's healing the nobleman's son.

Explanation of the Miraculous Event

The nobleman initiated the miraculous events requesting Jesus to travel from Cana of Galilee to Capernaum to heal his son, who was at the point of death (4:47). John does not tell us the details of the nobleman's son's sickness, but he does imply that this nobleman has sufficient faith in Jesus to travel from Capernaum to Cana to get His help. Wiersbe states, "This man began with *crisis faith*. He was about to lose his son, and he had no other recourse but the Lord Jesus Christ."[101] This nobleman is not alone in crisis faith; others came seeking Jesus's help out of a crisis faith (Centurion, Matt. 8:5–13, Luke 7:1–10; Syrophoenician woman, Matt. 15:21–28, Mark 7:24–30). Individuals who work in ministry can probably also

---

[100] Kostenberger, *Encountering John*, 60.
[101] Wiersbe, 303.

attest to people coming to them and the religious institutions out of a crisis faith.

The response of Jesus to the nobleman's request (4:48) at face value seems to be abrupt and harsh. O'Day and Hylen contend that "the 'you' of this verse is a second-person plural. John may have the reader of the Gospel in mind here as much as the characters in the story."[102] I agree that the "you people" (4:48) is a plural expression for multiple individuals instead of just a single person such as the nobleman. John seems to be hinting at the divine knowledge and ability of Jesus to discern the heart and desire of the people to see signs and wonders. Hughes supports the concept of seeing and then believing:

> With unerring accuracy, our Lord put his finger on the weakness of the people's faith. They were following Jesus as if he were a religious sideshow. "Hurry, hurry, don't miss the latest miracle! Get your popcorn here. Crowd in close, folks, so you can see the new added-appendage miracle." There was such an extreme focus on signs and wonders that the people were missing his real identity.[103]

Based on the words of Jesus in 4:48, the people of Judea and Galilee seemed to be preoccupied with seeing signs and wonders. This is directly related to the concept of seeing and believing, which was later demonstrated by the Lord's disciple Thomas in 20:25: "Unless I see in His hands the print of the nails and put my finger into the print of the nails, and put my hand into His side, I will not believe." Therefore, this philosophy of seeing and believing is a character trait of the lost world and the religious community.

---

[102] Gail R. O'Day and Susan E. Hylen, *John* (Louisville, KY: Westminster John Knox Press, 2006), 59.

[103] R. K. Hughes, *John: That You May Believe* (Wheaton, IL: Crossway Books, 1999), 139–140.

Edersheim advocates that Jesus reproved the request to come to Capernaum to heal the nobleman's son, but not necessarily the request to heal him.[104]

> That request argued ignorance of the real character of the Christ as if He were either merely a Rabbi endowed with special power or else a miracle-monger. What He intended to teach this man was that He, Who had life in Himself, could restore life at a distance as easily as by His Presence; by the word of His Power as readily as by personal application.[105]

The nobleman, in some respects, is comparable to the Syrophoenician woman in that he does not give up on his attempt to get Jesus to come and heal his son. It is a persistent faith, and yet it is misdirected in that he believes Jesus must be present to heal his son. The nobleman's statement, "Sir, come down before my child dies!" (4:49) suggests Jesus must be present to heal the child before death occurs.

Jesus simply responds to the nobleman by saying, "Go your way: your son lives" (4:49), without any other explanation or confirmation of His words. The power of His words was just as effective as in the first miracle of turning water into wine. In this situation, the power of Jesus's words extends beyond the immediate environment in Cana of Galilee to Capernaum, approximately fifteen miles away. Gromacki wrote about Jesus's power being "the source of life, He could give life to one who was about to die. It also proved the power of His word in that the son was healed the very moment Christ spoke miles away."[106] In actuality, Jesus gave a partial granting of the request in that He healed the son but did not go to Capernaum. Hughes states that

---

[104] Edersheim, *The Life and Times of Jesus the Messiah*, 425.

[105] Ibid.

[106] R. G. Gromacki, *New Testament Survey* (Grand Rapids, MI: Baker Academic, 1974), 140.

Jesus "gave the man no sign! The only thing he gave the man was his word. Our gracious Savior was attempting to elevate the nobleman to a higher faith."[107] O'Day and Hylen argue that "the royal official believes Jesus' word of life and promise before any results are known (v 50b); his immediate response to Jesus' instructions are evidence of his faith."[108]

The nobleman's response is critical regarding his faith in the word of Jesus; however, it is independent of the miracle itself. The nobleman distinguishes himself from other Galileans who requested signs and wonders (v. 48). He simply accepts the word from Jesus and goes away.[109] We will move to a discussion of similar miracles of this nature.

Other Miracles Similar to the Healing of the Nobleman's Son

I want to assert from the outset that the nobleman's son's healing is unique compared to the other healing miracles in the Synoptics and other historical records of healings. Let's begin with the Synoptic scriptures, of which McFadyen suggests that "the story about the official's boy healed at a distance (vv. 46–53) can be compared to Luke 7:4–10."[110] Bultmann maintains that the "story is based on Matt. 8:5–13 and Luke 7:1–10 with a few discrepancies."[111] I believe the discrepancies in the stories outweigh the similarities and refute the theory that the narrative in John was "reshaped under the influence of the Christian mission and its terminology."[112]

---

[107] Hughes, 140–141.

[108] O'Day and Hylen, 59.

[109] Carson, 239.

[110] P. McFadyen, *Open Door on John: A Gospel for Our Time* (London: Triangle, 1998), 27.

[111] Bultmann, 204.

[112] Ibid., 208–209.

Consider a few differences in these narratives:

1) Jesus is in Capernaum in Matthew 8:5–13 and Luke 7:1–10, whereas in John, He is in Cana of Galilee.

2) The centurion's servant is sick in Matthew and Luke, whereas the nobleman's son is sick in John.

3) The centurion in the Synoptics states his unworthiness for Jesus to come to his house but instead requests that Jesus "speak a word" (Matt.8:8; Luke 7:7). Jesus consents to go to the centurion's house, whereas in John, the nobleman begs Jesus to come to his house (John 7:49), and his request is denied.

4) Both the centurion and the nobleman demonstrate a level of faith; however, the centurion expresses faith before Jesus speaks a word of healing to his servant.

Brown also argues that the healing of the nobleman's son is a third variant of the centurion's boy in Matthew and Luke with minor details.[113] However, Kostenberger contends that while the story is similar to the Synoptic narratives in Matthew 8:5–13 and Luke 7:1–10, the nobleman's son in John 4:46–54 differs from the Gentile centurion.[114] I agree with Kostenberger, and even Carson concurs that the nobleman's son story differs from the Synoptic Gospels.[115]

The uniqueness of Jesus's healing the nobleman's son is further illustrated by the distance between Cana of Galilee and Capernaum, plus the fact that Jesus does not pray to anyone but merely speaks a word. The journey (distance and terrain) between these cities would have been rough travel, but this only magnifies the nobleman's request, who is desperate for help. The distance and terrain were not a problem for the power of Jesus. Keener comments that the

---

[113] Brown, *The Gospels and the Epistle of John*, 38–39.

[114] Kostenberger, *Encountering John*, 75.

[115] Carson, 234.

narratives of the centurion, the nobleman, and the Syrophoenician bolster the miraculous concept of long-distance healing.[116] In essence, the distance healing by Jesus supports the premise stated in John's purpose for writing the gospel (21:31).

Other historical records such as the Talmud record "various cases in which those seriously ill, and even at the point of death, were restored by the prayers of celebrated Rabbis."[117] It would not be uncommon for a Jew or even an informed Gentile to request healing prayers from a rabbi. Edersheim illustrates from the Talmud:

> When the son of Rabban Gamaliel was dangerously ill, he sent two of his disciples to one Chanina ben Dosa to entreat his prayers for the restoration of his son. On this, Chanina is said to have gone up to the *Aliyah* (upper chamber) to pray. On his return, he assured the messengers that the young man was restored, grounding his confidence, not on the possession of any prophetic gift, but on the circumstance that he knew his request was answered, from the freedom he had in prayer. The messengers noted down the hour, and on their arrival at the house of Gamaliel found that at that very hour, "the fever left him, and he asked for water."[118]

The uniqueness of Jesus's healing is that He did not have to pray to anyone or intercede on their behalf. John implies in this healing narrative that the spoken word of Jesus is a product of 1:4: "In Him was life, and the life was the light of men." Gromack wrote of Jesus, "As the source of life, He could give life to one who was about to die."[119] In essence, the nobleman's son was healed from a distance because of the words spoken by Jesus and not because Jesus was an

---

[116] Keener, 632.

[117] Edersheim, *The Life and Times of Jesus the Messiah*, 424.

[118] Ibid.

[119] Gromacki, 140.

intercessor praying to God for healing. Let us now turn to the impact of this miracle on the nobleman, his son, and his household.

Impact of the Miracle on the Nobleman, Son, and Household

The testimony of the miracle's impact on the nobleman is found in 4:50b: "So the man believed the word that Jesus spoke to him, and he went his way." Hughes says that "Jesus' words would lift the man to new levels of faith—and likewise anyone else who would listen and respond."[120] It is a clear case of this nobleman trusting the words of Jesus in that he does not continue to ask Jesus to come down to heal his son. His trust is further demonstrated by his obedience to the words of Jesus, "Go your way"; in the next verse, John tells us the nobleman is going down and meets his servants (4:51). John does not tell us the activities of the nobleman between his meeting with Jesus ("yesterday," 4:51–52) and his meeting with the servants while going down to Capernaum. We will not attempt to speculate on the activities of the nobleman after his encounter with Jesus beyond saying that his actions were in line with his trust in the words of Jesus for his son's life.

The servants of the nobleman testify to the nobleman in 4:51, "Your son lives!" Michaels advocates that the servants' testimony is important because it gives a precise time linking the recovery of the nobleman's son and the spoken words of Jesus.[121] After a brief inquiry in 4:52–53, we can conclude that the servants, as members of the household, make the connection between the spoken words of Jesus and the healed son. In todays' society, the faith of the head of household would rarely prompt the whole family to believe in Jesus. Keener gives insight concerning families during this era: "The Roman world expected families to share the faith of the head of the

---

[120] Hughes, 139–140.
[121] Michaels, 282.

household, and while exceptions to this expectation were frequent, they remained a minority of instances."[122] The New Testament writers share several illustrations whereby all in the household were believers due to the faith of the head of household (Acts 10:2; 11:14; 16:15, 31–14; 18:8). Therefore, the singular faith of the whole household was a common practice during this period in history.

The son of the nobleman is a silent witness and yet a crucial benefactor to the healing power of Jesus. His recovery confirmed the faith of the father and his household. Hughes insists that Christ's miracles were performed to make faith alive.[123] Perhaps I should mention that, too often in religious settings, the individual's faith is suggested as the crucial factor for healing. But John is silent on the faith of the nobleman's son before his recovery. The father's little faith was exercised, but the son's faith was assumed after the healing. Let us now look at the impact of this miracle on the early and present-day church.

Impact of the Miracle on the Church (Early and Present-Day)

The impact of this miracle of healing on the early and present-day church is probably one of speculation based on historical attitudes toward Jesus and then assumptions and hope in Jesus for the current-day church. Let us begin with nonbiblical literature describing the Jewish perception of Jesus. Riggans contends, "There is hardly any actual reference to Jesus in the literature of Talmudic times, which is to say, the first six centuries of the Common Era."[124] Riggans goes on to state,

---

[122] Keener, 632.

[123] Hughes, 139–140.

[124] W. Riggans, "The Jewish Reclamation of Jesus and Its Implications for Jewish-Christian Relations," *Themelios* 18, no. 1 (1992): 10.

The lack of reference to Jesus and the birth and growth of the church must be the result of a conscious decision to avoid, and indeed prevent, discussions about Jesus in the Jewish community. What mention there is of Jesus, or even of those Jewish people who became his followers, is further differentiated by being usually ascribed to the period of the Amoraim (*c.* 200–500) rather than the Tannaim (first and second centuries). In other words, the gospels are the only first-century documents that give us accounts of the early Jewish reaction to Jesus.[125]

Suppose we support Riggans's opinion that the Gospels are the primary documents to gauge the people's reaction. In that case, I must speculate briefly on the reaction to miracles during the time of Jesus Christ and why I believe this impacts the church. The Synoptics provide a general audience reaction to the miracles of Jesus, and I believe this is true for John's gospel as well:

1) Mark 4:41—After Jesus calmed the storm, the disciples "feared exceedingly."
2) Mark 5:15—After Jesus cast the demons out of the man, the people were afraid and asked Jesus to leave.
3) Mark 5:42—After Jesus raised the little girl, "they were overcome with great amazement."
4) John 5:15–18—The Jews sought to kill Jesus for healing the lame man on the Sabbath day.
5) John 6:14—The men fed by the fish and loaves of bread believed Jesus was the Prophet.
6) John 9:38—The blind man made well believed and worshiped Jesus.

---

[125] Riggans, 10.

Leavell concludes that the audience's response to miracles performed by Jesus seems to be fear, trembling, and amazement, and "this seems to be the natural reaction to the miraculous ministry of our Lord, both then and now. This fear hardens some persons and makes them cynical and doubtful. It warms the hearts of others and makes them believe more strongly."[126] Redford mentions as well that "the people present *praised God*, but probably did not grasp the full implications of what they had just witnessed."[127] On the other hand, the religious leaders left the miracle scenes frustrated and more determined to kill Jesus (John 5:18).

The present-day church seems to view the miracle of the healing of the nobleman's son as confirmation that Jesus does not have to be in the area to restore health to sick bodies. The message of the church always links Jesus with life and especially eternal life (10:10). Perhaps this is a play on words for the reaction of the current church in that *Son* and *life* always go together.[128] Wiersbe's commentary on this narrative applies to today's ministry work: the nobleman began with crisis faith and then moved to confident faith, followed by confirmed faith, and then contagious faith.[129] John's insertion of this distance healing miracle story is to make our faith come alive.[130]

In the gospel of John, the religious leaders seem to have a less positive reaction to the miracles and a more negative reaction concerning the fact that Jesus healed on the Sabbath or positioned Himself with God, which they consider blasphemy. This will be discussed more in the next chapter, about Jesus healing the man at the pool of Bethesda. There is still the question of whether this

---

[126] L. P. Leavell, "Mark," in *The Teacher's Bible Commentary*, eds. H. F. Paschall and H. H. Hobbs, (Nashville: Broadman and Holman Publishers, 1972), 623.

[127] D. Redford, *The Life and Ministry of Jesus: The Gospels*, Vol. 1 (Cincinnati: Standard Pub., 2007), 127–128.

[128] Michaels, 285.

[129] Wiersbe, 303.

[130] Hughes, 139–140.

miracle of the healing of the nobleman's son provides sufficient proof that Jesus is the Son of God, and we will address this next.

Whether This Miracle Provides Sufficient Proof that Jesus Is the Son of God

I believe this sign gives sufficient reason to believe Jesus is the Son of God for two primary reasons:

1) Jesus's healing of the nobleman's son is unique in that Jesus was in Cana of Galilee while the nobleman's sick son was in Capernaum. The distance between Jesus and the nobleman's son is repeatedly emphasized by the nobleman's requesting Jesus to "come down" to Capernaum. Other healings within the New Testament scriptures position the intermediary in an area close to the person in need, such as Acts 3:4–8, when Peter healed the lame man; 5:16, when Peter healed a multitude of sick people; and 9:33–35, when Peter healed Aeneas, who had been sick for eight years. In these healing stories, the sick people were in proximity to those individuals requesting the power of God for their healing. However, Jesus illustrates in this narrative of the nobleman's son that distance is not a limitation with God because of the power of His spoken word.

2) Jesus's healing of the nobleman's son is unique because He does not pray to God the Father but merely speaks a word of life (1:4). As Gromacki states about Jesus: "As the source of life, He could give life to one who was about to die. It also proved the power of His word in that the son was healed the very moment Christ spoke miles away."[131] Other healing

---

[131] Gromacki, 140.

stories, such as Chanina ben Dosa,[132] are illustrations of people praying to God as intercessors. Even the previous examples from the Acts of the Apostles are evidence of successful intercessors. However, Jesus does not pray as an intercessor but speaks life when He says, "Go your way; your son lives" (4:50). Neyrey suggests that Jesus responds to the nobleman on His terms, ultimately bringing about acknowledgment and faith in His name.[133] This healing narrative and the power demonstrated by Jesus ties very nicely with the prologue (1:4) and John's expressed purpose in 20:31. Let us proceed to the next chapter, wherein Jesus heals a man at the pool of Bethesda.

---

[132] Edersheim, *The Life and Times of Jesus the Messiah*, 424.
[133] Neyrey, 100.

CHAPTER 5

Jesus Heals the Man at the Pool of Bethesda

Background Information

John chapter 5 tells the reader that Jesus went up to Jerusalem for a feast of the Jews; however, the text does not tell us which feast was celebrated. Utley advocates that "there were three annual feast days which were mandatory for Jewish males to attend if at all possible (cf. Lev. 23): (1) Passover; (2) Pentecost, and (3) the Feast of the Tabernacle."[134] We will not speculate on which feast Jesus was attending because this information is not critical to the narrative of the man's healing at the pool of Bethesda. Identifying the feast is critical only if we are researching the length of Jesus's ministry on earth. John identifies three separate Passovers, which would account for a three-year ministry: John 2:13, 6:4, 11:55, and 12:1. What is

---

[134] R. J. Utley, *The Beloved Disciple's Memoirs and Letters: The Gospel of John, I, II, and III John*, Vol. 4 (Marshall, TX: Bible Lessons International, 1999), 50.

vital is the day of the week in which the healing takes place, and we will discuss the impact of healing on the Sabbath day.

The city of Jerusalem is known for being the religious center for the Jewish nation because it was chosen by God (1 Kings 11:36). Lohse and Fohrer state that "the name ירושלם ("Jerusalem") is found 660 times in the OT."[135] The city of Jerusalem was originally a Canaanite city, based on Joshua 10:1, but later became known as the capital of the Davidic reign and also called the city of David (2 Samuel 5—1 Kings 11).[136] The progression of Jesus's ministry as the One sent by the Father would prompt Him to visit Jerusalem on feast days; however, this visit encompasses more than just an annual feast.

The setting for this miracle of healing is in Jerusalem by the pool at the sheep gate, which "was on the northeast part of the wall of Jerusalem. It is mentioned in Nehemiah's rededication and reconstruction of the walls of the city (cf. Neh. 3:1, 32; 12:39)."[137] It is speculated that the purpose of the sheep gate was to allow sheep entrance into the temple for sacrifice.[138] There has been a recent archaeological discovery of a large pool near the gate where sheep were brought to the temple.[139] Perhaps the fact that Jesus visits the sheep gate is appropriate as the sent One who will later in John's gospel be sacrificed on behalf of the people.

The pool of Bethesda has generated numerous research opinions concerning its spelling and purpose. I want to look at several of these concerning the pool of Bethesda and the audience's beliefs regarding

---

[135] E. Lohse, and G. Fohrer, "Σιών, Ἰερουσαλήμ, Ἱεροσόλυμα, Ἱεροσολυμίτης," in *Theological Dictionary of the New Testament*, eds. G. Kittel, G. W. Bromiley, and G. Friedrich, Electronic ed., Vol. 7 (Grand Rapids, MI: Eerdmans, 1964), 295–296.

[136] Ibid.

[137] Utley, 50.

[138] *Holman Illustrated Bible Dictionary*, s.v. "sheep gate," eds. C. Brand, C. Draper, A. England, S. Bond, E. R. Clendenen, and T. C. Butler (Nashville, TN: Holman Bible Publishers, 2003), 1479.

[139] Brown, *The Gospel and Epistles of John*, 39–40.

the healing water. *Bethesda* is quite possibly the proper name as opposed to *Bezatha* or *Bethsaida*.[140] Utley writes concerning the various spellings of the name,

> Josephus also called it by the Hebrew name "Bethzatha," which was the name for this section of Jerusalem. It is also called "Bethsaida" in Greek manuscripts. The Qumram copper scrolls called it "Bethesda," which means "house of mercy" or "house of double spring." Today it is known as St. Anne's pool(s).[141]

Edersheim argues from a linguistic viewpoint that

> the name Bethesda might combine, according to a not uncommon Rabbinic practice, the Hebrew *Beth* with some Aramaised form derived from the Greek word ζέω, "to boil" or "bubble up" (subst. ζέσις); in which case it would mean "the House of Bubbling-up," viz. water.[142]

Thompson also supports the name *Bethesda* in his writing that "this 1st-century reference in the Copper Scroll to the name 'Bethesda' in relation to what appears to be a pool with two basins lends weight to this spelling."[143] The consensus of my research favors the spelling of the pool as *Bethesda*.

John informs the reader that the pool has five porches where sick and injured people wait for the moving of the water. Hughes speculates that hundreds of people came from the countryside to be healed, and the porches were built probably with a monetary donation from someone who was thrilled with what was taking

---

[140] Ibid.

[141] Utley, 50.

[142] Edersheim, *The Life and Times of Jesus the Messiah*, 462–463.

[143] Robin Thompson, "Healing at the Pool of Bethesda: A Challenge to Asclepius?" *Bulletin for Biblical Research* 27, no. 1 (2017): 68.

place at the pool.[144] Michaels also tells us that "the 'five porticoes,' or covered colonnades, should not be interpreted allegorically, any more than the 'six stone water jars' at Cana (2:6) or the Samaritan woman's 'five husbands' (4:18)."[145] The porches themselves, which function as covering for the sick and injured waiting for the stirring of the water (5:3), are not critical for further discussion; however, the reason that sick and injured people assembled at the pool of Bethesda warrants more attention. John 5:4 provides the reason, but many theologians question the validity of this verse in terms of actuality versus mythology versus natural causes.

Let's address the actuality first. Hughes states that "with the Hebrew preoccupation with angelology, it is quite natural that a legend was born. We find this spurious teaching in the text of the older New Testament translations, though not in the earliest manuscripts."[146] Michaels also supports the theory that the text in 5:4 was added to explain why many people, especially the sick man, were at the pool (5:7).[147] The New International Version omits the words of 5:3, beginning with "waiting for the moving of the water," and picks up again with verse 5. Other translations such as the King James Version (KJV) and New King James Version (NKJV) insert a Nestle-Aland Greek New Testament and United Bible Societies (NU) note in the margin regarding the words omitted. Thompson notes that "the earliest and best manuscripts omit both 5:3b–4."[148]

The mythology may help explain why these sick and injured people would gather at the pool. Keener implies that it was common practice for pagans to reuse earlier sanctuaries or sacred places.[149] Moloney supports this concept by stating that "the pool at Bethesda was

---

[144] Hughes, 145–146.

[145] Michaels, 289.

[146] Hughes, 146.

[147] Michaels, 290–291.

[148] Thompson, 76.

[149] Keener, 638.

known for pagan healing—probably back to the Canaanite times."[150] Witherington adds, "This story reveals the quiet desperation of people with ongoing illnesses in an age when medicine was either nonexistent or usually ineffective."[151] It is conceivable that multitudes of people with illnesses would camp out at the pool of Bethesda to wait on the moving of the water, which conceivably could have been based on mythology. Thompson suggests that this healing narrative was included to

> challenge the great Greco-Roman god of healing, for even years later the early church fathers found that in Asclepius they faced their strongest enemy, the most dangerous antagonist of their Master. The worship of Asclepius began in the late 6th century BC and resulted in Asclepius becoming the most important god of healing in the Greco-Roman world.[152]

Koester argues against 5:4 because "these practices are not well attested in Jewish sources, which commonly connected healing with prayer to God—and the God of Israel did not reserve his favor for those who were best able to help themselves."[153] Perhaps this is where we get the nonscriptural phrase "God helps those who help themselves." Lange, however, argues,

> According to the Jewish popular conception there was a personal angel who produced the moving of the water. John found the conception and admitted it in his narrative, translating in his own mind the personal angel into a symbolical angel, or a distinct divine operation, *i.e.*, in reference to such facts, for in a higher sphere he well knew

---

[150] Moloney, 168.

[151] Witherington, *John's Wisdom*, 137.

[152] Thompson, 66–77.

[153] Craig R. Koester, *Symbolism in the Fourth Gospel: Meaning, Mystery, Community* (Minneapolis: Fortress, 1995), 53.

the personal angels. He could leave the reader to adjust the passage according to chapter 1:51.[154]

The last reason I want to offer for many of the people remaining at the pool could be the natural underground springs swelling up and causing the water to move. Edersheim states definitively,

> This bubbling up of the water was, of course, due not to supernatural but to physical causes. Such intermittent springs are not uncommon, and to this day the so-called "Fountain of the Virgin" in Jerusalem exhibits the same phenomenon. It is scarcely necessary to say, that the Gospel-narrative does not ascribe this "troubling of the waters" to Angelic agency, nor endorses the belief, that only the first who afterwards entered them, could be healed. This was evidently the belief of the impotent man, as of all the waiting multitude.[155]

Hughes supports Edersheim's position that the pool at Bethesda "periodically rippled because of a subterranean spring, and no doubt usually someone who had a disease was in the pool when the water moved."[156] If such an individual were made better while in the pool, then the news of a miraculous pool would spread like wildfire.

The theological debate of whether John 5:3b–4 should or should not be omitted will probably continue for some years, as will the question of whether the water bubbled up due to underground springs or the divine intervention of an angel. We will not attempt to resolve these questions since the answers do not validate the miraculous sign of Jesus's healing the man at the pool of Bethesda. Let us now consider the characters involved in the narrative.

---

[154] J. P. Lange and P. Schaff, *A Commentary on the Holy Scriptures: John* (Bellingham, WA: Logos Bible Software, 2008), 183.

[155] Edersheim, *The Life and Times of Jesus the Messiah*, 463.

[156] Hughes, 145–146.

Characters Involved

Two main characters are involved in the man's healing at the pool of Bethesda: Jesus and the man with an infirmity. The multitude of sick, blind, and paralyzed people merely make up a supporting cast; John does not inform us of their participation, validation of the miracle, or any confrontation with Jesus or the man. The Jews in 5:10 are representatives of the Jewish authority who were more interested in the observance of the Sabbath day than the man healed from his infirmity. The Jews' question to the man prompts the confrontation with Jesus in the discourse from 5:16–47. This discussion is an aftermath of the miracle itself and indirectly part of the validation of the healing.

Jesus is the primary character in this narrative as He is visiting Jerusalem during the Jewish feast. Hughes contends, "On this occasion our Lord was alone. Without his disciples Jesus could virtually travel incognito."[157] Perhaps this is why the multitude and the man with an infirmity did not recognize Jesus (5:13). Surely others with the multitude would have called out to Jesus if they had known Him. Bultmann advocates that the healing is secondary to the fact that Jesus is revealing Himself as Lord of the Sabbath and His relationship with the Father. The law of the Sabbath does not bind Jesus from being a revealer of the Father.[158]

Considering Thompson's opinion regarding the popularity of the Greco-Roman cult of Asclepius being able to heal sick people, it makes sense that Jesus would come to this pool to demonstrate the power of God over the superstitious beliefs in Asclepius.[159] Culpepper notes that Jesus shows assertiveness in His dialogue despite the man's endless excuses.[160] Moloney adds that Jesus not only initiates the

---

[157] Hughes, 146.
[158] Bultmann, 244.
[159] Thompson, 65–84.
[160] Culpepper, *The Gospel and Letters of John*, 150.

confrontation with the man but uses His divine knowledge of the man's condition (5:6) to question him and generate dialogue.[161] I see intentional steps by Jesus to perform this miracle of healing as a sign of His power and authority.

The man with the infirmity is unnamed; however, "the mention of the length of the man's illness (thirty-eight years, v. 5) emphasizes the incurable nature of the man's condition."[162] Lange and Schaff write of the allegory of this man's sickness being "a symbol of the Jewish nation and in the thirty-eight years of his sickness a symbol of the thirty-eight years which Israel spent under the bane in the wilderness (I. 300 f.)."[163] Carson argues that there is no intertwining symbolism between the events of the wilderness experience and the length of time the man at the pool had been ill.[164] The question of the allegory is debatable, but his length of illness is reflective of his incurable condition and the hopelessness of his predicament. Let us now address the events of the miracle of the healing at the pool of Bethesda.

Explanation of the Miracle

After verses 1–5, wherein John provides background information for the miraculous event, he wrote in verse 6 of the sovereignty and omniscience (all-knowing) of Jesus to see and identify this man who had been suffering for a long time in his condition. O'Day and Hylen remind us that, whereas the nobleman knows Jesus (4:47), this sick man at the pool does not. John writes in 5:13 that this man had no prior knowledge of the identity of Jesus.[165] This man does not call out to Jesus for help. The sovereign choice of Jesus instigates the help

---

[161] Moloney, 168.

[162] O'Day and Hylen, 63.

[163] Lange and Schaff, 183.

[164] Carson, 242.

[165] O'Day and Hylen, 64.

for this man's condition in 5:6. The miraculous sign is an excellent follow-up to Jesus's initiative in chapter 4 with the Samaritan woman when He introduces Himself in a conversation with an unknown woman to reveal Himself and His relationship with the Father.

Jesus asks in 5:6, "Do you want to be made well?" The question could have been asked because an infirmity dictated the life of an infirm person.[166] The Scriptures normally characterized people with infirmities, particularly blind people, as beggars (Mark 10:46; John 9:8; Acts 3:2–3). Lange and Schaff suggest that "the question of Jesus, addressed to the cripple's desire for health, was a proof of sympathy with his sufferings, and kindled a spark of hope when on the brink of despair, and thus naturally prepared the way for his cure."[167] While Jesus's question seems to point to an obvious answer, perhaps this is another illustration of Jesus's presenting a clarifying question for the mind and soul. The question has a psychological impact on the mind, which is the first step toward wholeness.[168]

The sick man's response in 5:7 does not specifically answer Jesus's question but simply offers excuses for his inability to get in the pool first and be healed. When we consider that his response to Jesus is based upon the popular belief that only the first person into the pool after the waters have been disturbed would be miraculously healed, we can see the correlation to Jesus's question in 5:6.[169] The man's response indicates that he could not see past the water as the instrument of healing.[170] Witherington supports this opinion when he writes, "The man is not making a request for a cure from Jesus; he is not even thinking in those terms. He assumes that if there is to be a cure, it will come from the magical waters when they are moved."[171]

---

[166] Keener, 640.

[167] Lange and Schaff, 184.

[168] Carson, 243.

[169] Ibid.

[170] Kostenberger, 180.

[171] Witherington, *John's Wisdom*, 137.

This man's response to Jesus is not based upon any prior knowledge of Jesus but rather on his perceived hope for healing in the water. He is not fortunate like the paralytic man in Mark 2:1–12, who had four faithful men to help him; he is all alone in a desperate situation.

Jesus's statement (5:8) to the sick man bypasses engaging in conversation about the water. He simply states, "Rise, take up your bed and walk." John informs his readers that after Jesus speaks these words, the man is immediately healed. The power of the spoken word by Jesus supersedes the need for human intervention and the alleged healing springs of water.[172] O'Day and Hylen also support this position in that Jesus's command removed the need for the pool or human assistance to get in it.[173] The author, John, is no doubt trying to get his readers to see the power of the spoken word coming from Jesus just as other illustrations in the Synoptics (Matt. 9:6; Mark 2:9; Luke 5:24). The miraculous sign of the healing of the sick man at the pool of Bethesda is complete; however, the impact of this miracle concerning the faith of the man and the Jews warrants further discussion.

Impact of the Miracle on the Man and the Jews

There is an implied faith of the sick man in that he obeys the command of Jesus and picks up his mat and walks. John, however, does not tell us that the healed man had faith in Jesus, especially since he did not know Jesus before the healing. Culpepper agrees with me that there is a limited amount of faith due to his obedience to Jesus.[174] Brown suggests that there is no prerequisite of faith, especially when considering passages like Matthew 9:22, Mark

---

[172] Kostenberger, 180.

[173] O'Day and Hylen, 64.

[174] Culpepper, *The Gospel and Letters of John*, 150.

10:52, Luke 17:19, and Luke 18:42, whereby Jesus states the impact of the person's faith.[175]

I contend that John's gospel does not tell us that this man came to know Jesus as the Christ and Son of God because of the miracle performed at the pool of Bethesda. Culpepper agrees with me: "He does not know who healed him until Jesus finds him (5:14). He absolves himself of suspicion by implicating Jesus (5:15). Nothing suggests that this man became a believer in Jesus."[176] In comparing this man with the leper in Luke 17:12–19, who returned to give glory to God, this man healed at the pool does not return to Jesus; on the contrary, Jesus finds him in the temple (5:14). Moloney suggests that the healed man does not move to faith in Jesus, and the miraculous sign did not affect his belief.[177]

The implied lack of faith from this man healed by Jesus raises the question of faith before healing. I tend to believe that this narrative is more about the revelation of Jesus Christ than the faith of the man healed. O'Day and Hylen state that "this healing challenges many assumptions popular today that establish faith as a prerequisite for healing. This story emphasizes Jesus as the healer and turns upside down the notion of the 'worthiness' of the one who is healed."[178] I must conclude that the healing miracle performed by Jesus did not impact this man's faith.

The Jews, as a representation of those in opposition to Jesus, are also not persuaded by the healing of the sick man. The healing miracle, per se, is of little or no concern. In essence, they are more concerned about who told the man to carry his bed on the Sabbath day, which was a violation of the law (Lev. 23:27–32). Brown argues,

---

[175] Brown, *The Gospel and Epistles of John*, 39–42.
[176] Culpepper, *The Gospel and Letters of John*, 150.
[177] Moloney, 169.
[178] O'Day and Hylen, 64.

Jesus does not justify His action on humanitarian grounds as in the Synoptics, but on the grounds to reveal His supreme authority. While the Biblical teaching is that God rested on the Sabbath, rabbis understood that God's providential maintenance of the universe continues even on the Sabbath. The implication is that Jesus is equal to God and points at His deity in giving life and judgment.[179]

Moloney agrees with Brown in stating about 5:17,

It is a statement of a relationship between Jesus and the Father. The Jews understand this correctly; no misunderstanding here. They understand that God is LORD of the Sabbath in that He can work on that day also plus, Jesus is claiming to be equal with God; therefore, He can perform work on the Sabbath.[180]

The remaining discussion within John 5:16–47 focuses on Jesus's relationship with the Father. So, in effect, the miracle of healing the sick man prompts the discussion of the breaking of the Sabbath day, which then acts as fuel for the discussion of Jesus's relationship with the Father for the purpose of revealing His identity. Bultmann comments that the Jews perceive Jesus's words as "insane blasphemy," and He is portrayed among "the great blasphemers, Hiram, and Nebuchadnezzar, Pharaoh and Joash, who made themselves equal with God."[181] These Jews are postured for an impasse and therefore do not believe in Jesus but seek to persecute and kill Him (5:16).

---

[179] Brown, *The Gospel and Epistles of John*, 39–42.
[180] Moloney, 170.
[181] Bultmann, 244.

Other Similar Miracles and the
Uniqueness of This Sign

I want to assert from the outset that the healing of the man at the pool of Bethesda is unique compared to other healing miracles in the Synoptics and pagan historical records of healings.

Several Synoptic healing narratives correlate with the healing performed by Jesus on the Sabbath day, such as Matthew 12:9–13; Mark 3:1–5; and Luke 6:6–10, 13:10–14, and 14:1–5. The healing in Mark 2:1–12 of the paralytic man has similarities in terms of the response of Jesus to the scribes (2:6) when He says, "Arise, take up your bed and walk." However, the objection of the scribes is not based on the Sabbath day but rather on Jesus's authority to forgive sins. Essentially this healing in Mark 2:1–12 focuses on the identity and authority of the Son of Man to forgive sin, and there is no indication of Sabbath day violations by Jesus or the four men previously carrying the paralytic man.

The healing location at the pool of Bethesda distinguishes it from other healings in that historically, this pool is believed to have been a large site used for pagan healings. Talbert's describes the pool as follows:

> It measures 165–220 feet wide by 315 feet long. It consists of a twin basin (one side for men, one for women) to which Herod had added five elaborate porticoes surrounding the four sides and dividing the two basins across the middle. Stairways in the corners permitted descent into the pool.[182]

We have commented in the background information section of the Greco-Roman cult of Asclepius, and now Klinger suggests

---

[182] C. H. Talbert, *Reading John: A Literary and Theological Commentary on the Fourth Gospel and the Johannine Epistles* (Macon, GA: Smyth and Helwys Publishing, 2005), 127.

it was the healing sanctuary of the god Eshmun in Afqa. Klinger suggests that the healing center at Bethesda was previously a pool for cult worship to a pagan healer-god. Suppose these theories of the pool being a pagan healing center are correct. In that case, it means that Jesus deliberately entered a pagan sanctuary for healing and performed a miracle there on the Sabbath day.

Keener argues that "Jesus replaces not only John's baptism (1:31–33), ritual purity (2:6), proselyte baptism (3:5), and the Samaritan water of Jacob's well (4:14) but also the water of a popular healing cult."[183] It was not uncommon for pagans to reuse earlier sanctuaries or sacred spaces, such as when Aelia Capitoline, for example, reused the Jerusalem temple site for a pagan one.[184] In essence, the uniqueness of this miraculous sign is in the location of the pool of Bethesda and the authority demonstrated by Jesus in the miracle. A person can believe the pool was previously used as a pagan sanctuary for healing, a hot spring from underneath the earth, or even the site of an angel periodically moving the water. In any situation, Jesus works in accord with His Father's will to exercise sovereign authority over extended illness regardless of the individual's faith or the day of the week. This leads us to the next discussion of the impact of this miraculous sign on the church.

Impact of the Miracle on the Church (Early and Present-Day)

The impact of this miracle on the church raises questions of the necessity of faith in healing. The sign also ties the knot stronger for believing the relationship between the Father and Jesus the Son.

---

183 Keener, 638.
184 Ibid.

The fact that this man had no faith before the healing must imply that the purpose of this story is to clarify the work of Jesus.[185] While the man does obey the words of Jesus, there is nothing in the text to suggest that he had faith prior to the spoken word of Jesus (5:7–9). In contrast to this narrative in John 5, numerous passages in the Synoptics show the necessity of faith (Matt. 9:22, 29, 15:28; Mark 2:5, 5:34, 10:52; Luke 5:20, 7:9, 50; 8:48; 17:19; 18:42).

Moloney, however, suggests that the man was healed before his obedience to the words of Jesus and that, furthermore, there is nothing in the text to suggest that this man moved to faith in Jesus (5:15).[186] When we compare this man in John 5 with the blind man in John 9, they are opposites in terms of their expressions of faith in Jesus. O'Day and Hylen add that this healing narrative challenges the assumption that faith is a prerequisite for healing.[187] The man's faith appears to be more in the water's motion than in Jesus (5:7). Perhaps this healing narrative is not to focus on the man's faith at the pool but rather the revelation of Jesus and the work He does in relationship to the Father. Bultmann supports this view by advocating that "the healing is secondary to the fact that Jesus is revealing Himself as Lord of the Sabbath and His relationship with the Father."[188] Therefore, I would advocate that faith was not a requirement in this healing because the objective was to reveal Jesus's relationship to the Father.

Bryan states that the healing at the pool of Bethesda "on the Sabbath functions as a sign of the unity between the actions of the Son and the Father."[189] When we review the narrative leading up to the miracle, we see that Jesus is in complete control. He initiates the conversation with the man after seeing and understanding his

---

[185] Brown, *The Gospel and Epistles of John*, 39–42.

[186] Moloney, 169.

[187] O'Day and Hylen, 64.

[188] Bultmann, 244.

[189] Steven M. Bryan, "Power in the Pool: The Healing of the Man at Bethesda and Jesus' Violation of the Sabbath," *Tyndale Bulletin* 54, no. 2 (2003): 8.

condition. The unanswered question in 5:6 ("Do you want to be made well?") does not hinder the healing miracle. John tells us in 5:9, "Immediately the man was made well," and we cannot help but see that his healing is due to the spoken word of Jesus. The power of the spoken word suggests the deity of Jesus as being equal to God and able to give life and pronounce judgment.[190] Clearly, in the discourse following the healing miracle, Jesus defends His action of healing on the Sabbath with the fact that the Father continues working as well (5:17), and He is simply doing what the Father does (5:19). Ryrie supports the spiritual aspect versus the physical healing in that these are

> not done primarily to benefit those who were healed and fed but to glorify God or to teach the disciples or to confirm His claims of deity. It is as if the actual physical benefit was secondary to the spiritual lessons intended, for indeed, His priorities were spiritual.[191]

Many at the pool of Bethesda were sick; however, Jesus chose to heal only one sick man.

> If Christ's purpose had been the healing of the sick, he would have healed them all. Thus, a miracle of healing today should not be expected when it is medically desirable but rather where the Word of God and his servant needs to be authenticated and illustrated, and such evidence is not already available in the Bible.[192]

---

[190] Brown, *The Gospel and Epistles of John*, 39–42.

[191] C. C. Ryrie, *Dr. Ryrie's Articles* (Bellingham, WA: Logos Bible Software, 2010), 137.

[192] D. T., "Health, Disease and Healing," in *New Bible Dictionary*, 3rd ed., eds. D. R. W. Wood, I. H. Marshall, A. R. Millard, J. I. Packer, and D. J. Wiseman (Downers Grove, IL: InterVarsity Press, 1996), 453.

The message to the present-day church is that Jesus is the giver of life, whether it is physical or spiritual. The healing of the sick man at the pool of Bethesda is an illustration of Jesus's giving physical life (1:4) just as the Father gives life. "The Word is the agent or instrument of bringing the world to life. Thus, Jesus is the agent of bringing life to the world, sustaining the world even on the Sabbath as does the Lord God of Israel."[193] Let us now consider whether this sign provides sufficient evidence of the deity of Jesus as the Son of God.

Whether This Sign Gives Sufficient Reason to Believe Jesus Is the Son of God

I believe this sign gives sufficient reason to believe Jesus is the Son of God for several reasons:

(1) The healing event is a product of Jesus. The man who had been sick for thirty-eight years does not know Jesus or request healing from Jesus. Jesus initially sees the man and sparks a conversation with him. Jesus ignores the man's excuse for not being healed by the stirring of the water, and then He speaks physical life into the man that enables him to stand up and take up his bed. The only aspect of this healing event attributed to the sick man is his obedience to the command of Jesus, which I also believe is a by-product of the spoken word of life. This healing is illustrative of the concept of salvation in that we cannot be saved without divine intervention. Spiritual salvation was also available when Jesus (5:14) found the man in the temple.

---

[193] M. M. Thompson, "Signs and Faith in the Fourth Gospel," *Bulletin for Biblical Research,* Vol. 1, (1991): 100.

(2) The physical healing and the availability for spiritual cleansing (5:14) can be attributed to Jesus's characteristics as the Son of God. This healing illustrates Jesus as being Lord of the Sabbath and directly related to God the Father. Kostenberger argues that

> if this were the Synoptic Gospels, the miracle itself would be sufficient to demonstrate Jesus' authority over sickness (cf. Mark 2:1–12) or his fulfillment of the messianic mission envisioned by Isaiah (Matt. 8:17; 12:18–21; Luke 4:18–19; cf. Isa. 42:1–4; 53:4; 58:6; 61:1–2). In John, however, the miracle is transmuted into a "sign" (possibly alluded to in 7:21–24), an act with inherent Christological symbolism.[194]

The Christological symbolism radiates that Jesus has within Himself the power of life (1:4) to heal without the need for moving water (5:7) or being restricted to certain days of the week. Jesus has this authority and power because He is the Son of God. This healing narrative fulfills the objective of John 20:31, "that you may believe that Jesus is the Christ, the Son of God, and that believing you may have life in His name." Let us now move to John 6:1–14, with Jesus feeding the multitude.

---

[194] Kostenberger, *Encountering John*, 79.

CHAPTER 6

Jesus Feeds the Five Thousand

Background Information

John begins chapter 6 by informing the reader that Jesus has traveled "over the Sea of Galilee, which is the Sea of Tiberias" (6:1). The setting for this miraculous sign is the Sea of Galilee, which is the Hellenistic name for the lake. During the Roman period, it was called the Sea of Tiberias due to Herod Antipas in 20 AD.[195] The Sea of Galilee is referred to in the Bible by various names: the Sea of Tiberias (6:1, 21:1), the Lake of Gennesaret (Luke 5:1), and the Sea of Chinnereth (Joshua 12:3, 13:27). Brochert gives insight into the Hebrew name *Gennesaret.*

> Luke (5:1) refers to the sea as Gennesaret from the Hebrew name Kinnereth/Chinnereth meaning "lyre" or "harp," which some have thought, with Josephus, was derived from the shape of the lake but may have originated from the

---

[195] Borchert, 250.

nearby Canaanite town Tell El-'Oreimeth, which was lyre-like in shape.[196]

The Sea of Galilee was described as "a harp-shaped freshwater lake about thirty-two miles around, located in northern Palestine."[197] Carver tells us that the Sea of Galilee was a nucleus for major economic traffic within the area, providing fresh water, vegetation, and fishing. The surrounding landscape produced food supplies for the Egyptian military while on distant campaigns.[198] John does not inform us how Jesus crossed the Sea of Galilee, but he does tell us that the people followed Him because they saw the "signs which He performed on those who were diseased" (6:2).

We can surmise that the multitude did not believe Jesus was the Christ, Son of God, especially considering 6:14, in that John offers insight into the purpose of the multitude seeking Jesus. John identifies only the number of men in the multitude, which was about five thousand 6:10). The parallel passages in Mark 6:44 and Luke 9:14 support the number of five thousand men. However, Matthew 14:21 expands the number of the multitude to be five thousand men plus women and children. Kostenberger advocates that the number of men combined with women and children could have been closer to twenty thousand.[199] The five thousand number in John's writing reflects many people who followed Jesus by boat or on foot because of the miracles performed.

The mountainside where Jesus sat with His disciples has much symbolism. Michaels suggests that this unnamed mountain implies a place of divine revelation, similar to two other mountain scenes

---

[196] Ibid., 251.

[197] M. A. Powell, "Zurishaddai," *The HarperCollins Bible Dictionary*, 3rd ed. (New York: HarperCollins, 2011).

[198] A. C. Carver, "Galilee, Sea of, Archaeology of," in *The Lexham Bible Dictionary*, eds. J. D. Barry, D. Bomar, D. R. Brown, R. Klippenstein, D. Mangum, C. Sinclair Wolcott, ... W. Widder, (Bellingham, WA: Lexham Press, 2016).

[199] Kostenberger, *John*, 202.

in Matthew's gospel (5:1, 15:29).[200] Kostenberger advocates that *mountainside* could simply refer to the high ground we know as the Golan Heights and not a specific mountain.[201] Regardless of whether John is trying to designate Jesus's location as being on an actual mountain or just a location in the hill country, the symbolism from other passages of scripture such as Matthew 5:1, 15:29, and 28:16 cannot be ignored as a place where Jesus met with His disciples, taught, and practiced kingdom principles.

Passover is the season in which this miraculous sign of feeding the five thousand occurs (6:4). Carson suggests that John mentions the nearness of Passover not so much for the chronological effect but for the theological significance.[202] "The Jewish Passover celebrated the exodus from Egypt. Intrinsic to the celebration was the slaughter of a lamb in each household, which they ate. In this Gospel, Jesus is the Lamb of God (1:29, 36)."[203] While the Passover recognized the time in history in which God saved His people from slavery, in John's gospel, it is the time for the ultimate sacrifice of the Lamb for the sins of the world (1:35). In the discourse following the miraculous feeding of the five thousand, Jesus elaborates on Himself as being the "living bread" (6:51) and on His "flesh" and "blood" being necessary food and drink (6:55) for life. In essence, Jesus was stating that He would be the Passover lamb offered on behalf of those who would believe in Him. This mention of the Passover season theologically ties the feeding of the five thousand to not only Moses in the wilderness as the lawgiver, but more so to the identity of Jesus, Himself as the grace provider. Let us now consider the characters involved in the miracle of feeding the five thousand.

---

[200] Michaels, 342.

[201] Kostenberger, *John*, 200.

[202] Carson, 268.

[203] Ibid.

Characters Involved

In contrast to the number of characters involved in the man's healing at the pool of Bethesda, this miraculous sign involves multiple characters with various roles: Jesus, Philip and Andrew, the lad, the multitude, and the disciples.

Jesus is the primary character involved in setting up the scene for the miracle (6:5), giving instructions before and after the performance of the miracle (6:10, 12). Jesus's role is essential in John's gospel to point the reader toward the objective in John 20:31. Culpepper argues that the steps of Jesus were preconceived and not dictated by the disciples or the multitude.[204] Whereas requestors prompt the first and second miracles performed by Jesus, the third and fourth miracles are initiated by Jesus in obedience to and for the revelation of the Father (6:29).

The multitude and the disciples are group characters in how they are identified in this narrative. Both the multitude and the disciples are participants and recipients of the miracle performed by Jesus. John does not identify the nationality of the multitude, and we will not engage in Jewish speculation based upon 6:4 and 6:14. The multitude has the initial characteristics of discipleship in that they follow Jesus; however, their motives for following Jesus are impure, so they remain potential disciples only. Keener cites "a critical motif in Johannine soteriology: it is not those who begin to follow Jesus, but those who persevere who remain his disciples (6:60–71)."[205] Except for Philip and Andrew, the disciples are unnamed, so we will say that they are involved in distributing the food and collecting the fragments (6:11–13). They are witnesses to the feeding miracle performed by Jesus.

Philip was one of the earliest disciples called by Jesus (1:43), and he, along with Andrew and Peter, was from the city of Bethsaida

---

[204] Culpepper, *The Gospels and the Letters of John*, 155.
[205] Keener, 665.

(1:44). John tells us that Philip was tested by Jesus (6:5), a common practice by the Lord toward those in ministry work. Keener speculates that Philip may have made a profession of faith in Jesus during the conversation recorded in 1:43–46, and now his faith is being tested.[206] The Old Testament has numerous passages stating that God tested His chosen people (Gen. 22:1—Abraham was tested; Exod. 16:4—the children of Israel were tested with manna, and Jeremiah 17:10—He tested the heart of people). Jesus is merely mirroring the pattern demonstrated by His Father when He tests Philip in 6:5–6.

Andrew is probably best known as being one of the original disciples and the first missionary of Jesus (1:35–40). Missionary-minded Andrew brought his brother Simon (later named Peter) to Jesus in John 1:41–42. It is implied in John 6:9 that Andrew brought the lad with the five barley loaves and two small fish to Jesus. Both Philip and Andrew are involved with Greeks attempting to see Jesus in John 12:20–22. Andrew's role in the fourth gospel seems to portray him as assisting in the work of the ministry, whether it is bringing someone to Jesus or simply helping the ministry effort. Perhaps in the current-day church, we could benefit from a few more Andrew-type followers.

Carson states, "The Greek word *paidarion*, rendered 'a boy', can refer to a young man or a young slave (cf. BAGD and MM, s. v.; NewDocs 1. $45)."[207] The best we can speculate is that this young un-named person, unaware of the pending miracle, willingly gave his lunch to Jesus for the glory of the Father. Let us now examine the miracle of feeding the five thousand.

---

[206] Ibid.
[207] Carson, 270.

Explanation of the Miracle

The fourth gospel author sets the scene by informing the reader that Jesus and His disciples are on the mountain after crossing the Sea of Galilee. We are told that a multitude has followed Jesus because of the signs of healing sick people. We can quickly get the impression that Jesus is in control of the circumstances leading up to the feeding miracle. David Sick advocates that "at nearly all the banquets Jesus attends in the gospels, he is a guest, not the host (John 2:2; Luke 7:36, 19:5)."[208] However, in this miracle story, Jesus appears to be the host from the very start, when He asked Philip a question (6:5), all the way to the finished activity of gathering up the fragments (6:12). Let's begin with the test question for Philip.

The testing question Jesus presents to Philip cannot be solved by the disciples because there was a problem of insufficient raw material to feed the multitude.[209] John tells us that the question was a test (6:6); however, it also suggests that Jesus demonstrates divine knowledge in arranging a situation whereby only He can resolve a material problem. In essence, Jesus probes the disciples' knowledge of the food problem before presenting a miraculous solution. Philip's response about eight months' wages (NIV 6:7) not being sufficient to buy enough bread indicates humans' limitation to solving this food shortage for the multitude.

Culpepper informs us that only John's writing describes the type of loaves as barley (poor people's food), which ripens earlier than wheat. Barley was also used to feed livestock in 1 Kings 4:28 and the miracle feeding performed by Elisha in 2 Kings 4:42–44. Andrew's input identifying a lad with five barley loaves and two small fish further illustrates the magnitude of what Jesus is about to perform as

---

[208] David H. Sick, "The Symposium of the 5,000," *The Journal of Theological Studies* NS 66, pt. 1, (April 2015): 1.

[209] Moloney, 198.

the host for this banquet. It is safe to say that barley was a common people's food and that this lad was a common person.

David Sick gives an interpretation of the small fish based upon James Davidson's work *Courtesans and Fishcakes*:

> The association of fish and οφα led to a specialized meaning of the word, probably prior to Plutarch's era, and that specialized meaning can be found in the account in the Gospel of John. The author of the fourth gospel changes the standard word for fish ιχθύς found in Mark (6:38, 41, 43), Matthew (14:17, 19), and Luke (9:13, 15) to ὀφάριον, the diminutive of οφον "relish" at 6:9 and 11. In John's account tile banqueters take "as much as they wanted from the little relishes/fishes."[210]

Keener suggests that the fish may have been dried.[211] Michaels argues that the fish were actual fish from the lake and not necessarily prepared as edible food.[212] I notice that in Michaels's reference, the word for fish was ὀφάριον, which agrees with Sick in that these small fish could perhaps be a topping for the loaves of bread. Whether it was literal fish or a relish-type topping, it was a minuscule amount to feed the multitude of five thousand men plus women and children.

Jesus gives additional evidence of being the host of this feeding banquet in 6:10 when He instructs the people to sit down in preparation for the meal. Their sitting on the grass implies it is the warm season when the miracle takes place, but it also prompts us to recall the similarity of Psalm 23:2: "He makes me to lie down in green pastures." Carson contends that the grass's green detail illustrates a literary detail and confirms that the event took place

---

[210] Sick, "The Symposium of the 5,000," 9.

[211] Keener, 666.

[212] Michaels, 347.

in March or April near the Passover season.[213] Elowsky also agrees with Carson in that grass was abundant but adds that "it was Nisan (more or less April) when the earth usually becomes adorned with growing weeds, especially in those regions with hotter weather."[214] The multitude sitting on the grass is more of a reclining position, and this alludes to the Passover (6:4) or being at a banquet or festival per the Greek custom.[215] The multitude is now prepared to experience a feeding miracle.

Jesus, again functioning as the host, takes the loaves and fish, gives thanks, and distributes them. It cannot be emphasized enough that Jesus gives thanks before distributing the bread and fish. Elowsky advocates that this illustration of thanksgiving before the meal is "to show that when we begin our meals, we ought to give thanks to God. He does not do this because he needs to, but to show in both the lesser and greater things it is fitting."[216] There is the question of whether Jesus gave the loaves and fish directly to the multitude or first to the disciples, and then the disciples distributed the food. John's writing agrees with the Synoptics (Matt. 14:19; Mark 6:41; Luke 9:16) in that He gave to the disciples, and they, in turn, gave to the multitude. John does not tell us that Jesus broke the bread as in the Synoptic Gospels; however, in 6:12, we can infer that the fragments are the result of broken bread.

The miracle per se can be suggested to have taken place after Jesus gave thanks (6:11) and before the disciples distributed to the multitude. The lavishness of this miraculous sign is the sufficiency of bread and fish for the multitude to eat and be filled, plus a symbolic twelve baskets of fragments over and above what was needed. This miraculous sign "shows Christ's ability to satisfy the hunger of men,

---

[213] Carson, 270.
[214] Elowsky, 213.
[215] Keener, 666.
[216] Elowsky, 214.

which is crassly misunderstood by the multitudes (6:1–15)."[217] Carson argues that John portrays that the five loaves of bread and two small fish were multiplied so that the five thousand men and the women and children were filled (6:12) as a miracle and not a Eucharistic mouthful.[218] I will discuss the symbolism of this miracle in terms of being a Eucharistic meal in the section dealing with the impact on the church.

Elowsky explains the miracle as occurring while the disciples are distributing the bread and fish. "While the apostles are dividing them, a succession of newly created portions passes—they cannot tell how—through their hands. The loaf which they are dividing does not grow smaller and yet their hands are continuously full of pieces."[219] Michaels disagrees and argues that, contrary to the other parallel stories in the Gospels, in John's record, Jesus distributes the food directly to the crowd instead of giving it to the disciples to distribute.[220] However, I believe that the opinion of Elowsky does not conflict with John's writing or the Synoptic Gospels. While the Nestle-Aland Greek New Testament and United Bible Societies (NU) omits Jesus's giving "to the disciples, and the disciples" (6:11) distribute to the multitude, it is reasonable to agree with the Synoptics that Jesus would utilize the disciples for dispensing the food to the five thousand as opposed to personally performing this task. There is some similarity in the concept of this miracle's food multiplication to that which occurred in the miracle of meal and oil for the widow at Zarephath in 1 Kings 17:14. As the need occurred for food, the supply was available in abundance. In essence, Jesus gave thanks, broke the bread and fish, and gave them to the disciples, and while they were

---

[217] Raymond E. Brown, "The Distinctives of John's Gospel," *Southwestern Journal of Theology* 8, no. 1 (Oct 1965): 31.

[218] Carson, 270.

[219] Elowsky, 214.

[220] Michaels, 349.

distributing them to the multitude, the disciples continuously had newly created bread and fish to dispense.

The fragments (6:12) are perhaps the result of what today we call leftovers from a dinner party. Collecting what was leftover at the end of the meal was a Jewish custom during this period.[221] John and the Synoptic Gospels do not tell us what became of the twelve baskets, and we will not speculate. We know that the miraculous creation of bread and fish in this narrative satisfied the multitude and provided a significant amount of food over and above what was needed.

O'Day and Hylen point out that "for most people in Rome's world, the food supply was unpredictable and inadequate; this caused pervasive undernourishment and resulted in diseases from both deficiency and contagion."[222] This miraculous feeding could be an illustration of Jesus's fulfilling Jeremiah 31:14 (NIV): "I will satisfy the priests with abundance, and my people will be filled with my bounty, declares the LORD." John tells us that the purpose for gathering the fragments is "so that nothing is lost" (6:12). While this statement is literally about the leftover food, it has spiritual implications for people in the body of Christ.

The spiritual implications of the bread and the fragments must be seen in reference to the discourse that follows this narrative. Keener argues that the bread cannot symbolize God's people but must be seen as the symbol of Jesus Christ alone (6:32–35, 41, 48, 50–51, 58).[223]

The disciples' obedience in gathering the fragments is noteworthy (6:13), and we would be wise to mirror this concept of not being wasteful in our daily lives. Kostenberger writes, "It was customary at Jewish meals to collect what was left over. Pieces of bread were not to be thrown around (b. *Ber.* 50b), and food the size of an olive or larger

---

[221] Carson, 271.

[222] O'Day and Hylen, *John*, 61.

[223] Keener, 669.

must be picked up (b. *Ber.* 52b)."[224] Jesus is showing the application of Jewish principles that were a part of the culture and times.

The contrast of twelve baskets of fragments compared to the lad's lunch of five loaves and two fish shows the power of Jesus to create and satisfy with relatively small things. John may write of the twelve baskets as being symbolic of the twelve tribes of Israel, about which Carson states that "the word for basket (*kophinos*) used in all four accounts of the feeding of the five thousand has peculiarly Jewish associations, whereas the basket (*spyris*) used in the feeding of the four thousand (Mt. 15:37; Mk. 8:8) does not."[225] If the reference is to the twelve tribes of Israel, then perhaps John tells us that the miraculous sign shows Jesus's ability to provide provisions for His chosen people. Let us now consider other feeding miracles similar to John's narrative.

Other Miracles Similar to the Feeding of the Five Thousand

The feeding of the five thousand was a reminder of the feeding of the children of Israel in the wilderness when the Lord gave them manna from heaven (Exodus 16). It is noteworthy to mention that in the narrative of feeding in the wilderness, Moses is not the provider or the host. In contrast, in John 6, Jesus is both provider and host, which points to a role like but superior to Moses. The children of Israel were told (Deut. 18:15) that the Lord would raise up a prophet like Moses, and John's feeding narrative informs the reader that the men who received the multiplied bread and fish recognized Jesus as "the Prophet who is to come into the world" (6:14). John the Baptist denied being the Prophet (1:21); however, the gospel is silent as to whether Jesus responded to these men's claims. We do know that

---

[224] Kostenberger, *John*, 202.
[225] Carson, 271.

Jesus perceived their intentions (6:15) and departed from them, whereas Moses remained with the children of Israel in the wilderness.

Another similar miracle can be cited in 2 Kings 4:42–44, whereby Elisha fed one hundred men with twenty loaves of barley bread and newly ripened grain. The servant of Elisha obeyed his instructions to "give it to the people that they may eat; for thus says the LORD" (2 Kings 4:43), the one hundred men were filled, and there were leftovers. Horst argues that the author of John "convincingly demonstrates that this story is based to a great extent upon postbiblical Jewish traditions concerning Elisha's feeding of 100 men with twenty loaves of bread (2 Kings 4:42–44)."[226]

I would admit that there are similarities between the Elisha feeding and the Jesus feeding in terms of both miracles' utilizing and multiplying barley loaves to feed more than the raw materials could satisfy. However, some major differences suggest the Jesus miracle is not dependent on the Elisha feeding. First, Elisha gives instructions to the servant based upon "thus says the LORD," whereas Jesus is the Lord and functions as the host and provider for the feeding of the five thousand. Second, the raw numbers involved in the miracles are so vastly different: Elisha used twenty loaves to feed one hundred men, while Jesus used five loaves plus two small fish for five thousand men, not including women and children. In essence, Jesus feeds and satisfies more people with fewer raw materials, and then there are twelve baskets of fragments remaining. Third, the Elisha feeding points to the Word of the Lord as the source of the miracle, whereas the feeding of the multitude in John's writing points to Jesus's identity as the Word that became flesh and dwelt among us (John 1:14).

Culpepper advocates that the feeding of the multitude in John points back to "Moses and Elisha and the people respond with the

---

[226] Pieter W. van der Horst, "Review of Aus, Roger D. Feeding the Five Thousand: Studies in the Judaic Background of Mark 6:30–44 par. and John 6:1–15." Novum testamentum 53, no. 4. Lanham, MD: University Press of America, 2010, 405–406.

confession that Jesus is 'indeed the prophet who is to come into the world,' recalling Moses's prophecy in Deuteronomy 18:15 and 18."[227] The focus of these feeding narratives is on the deity being the source or provider. John's narrative of the feeding of five thousand points us to the deity of Jesus in support of the purpose stated in 20:31.

The feeding of the five thousand is one of the few miraculous signs recorded in all four Gospels (Matt. 14:15–21; Mark 6:35–44; Luke 9:12–17; John 6:1–14). The basic flows of the narratives are similar in the Synoptics, whereby the writers tell us that the disciples want to send the multitude away instead of trying to meet their need for food. Jesus takes the initiative in all the Gospels as the host and provider of spiritual and material needs. All gospel narratives tell us that Jesus gave thanks before the distribution of the bread and fish. The Synoptics tell us that Jesus broke the bread and gave it to His disciples, who then gave it to the multitude. John's gospel excludes the breaking of the bread, and we must assume that the breaking of the bread occurred sometime between Jesus's giving it to the disciples and the disciples' giving it to the multitude (6:12–13). In all of the gospel narratives, the capacity of Jesus to take very little and do so much is indicative of His superabundant ability to feed and nourish people.[228] Let us now consider the impact of this feeding narrative on the audience.

Impact of the Miracle on the Audience

John 6:14 informs us that the men took notice of what Jesus had done as a sign and proclaimed Him as the anticipated Prophet. Moloney explains that the sign leads to a limited faith in which "the people professed Jesus as a prophet who is to come into the world.

---

[227] R. Alan Culpepper, "Cognition in John: The Johannine Signs as Recognition Scenes," *Perspective in Religious Studies* 35, no. 3 (2008): 251–260.
[228] O'Day and Hylen, 72.

They were looking for a figure who would satisfy their expectations—Jesus like a Moses-like prophet from the wilderness days."[229] John 6:2 tells us that the multitude followed Jesus because of the signs; now they witness Him multiplying bread and fish and conclude that He is the Prophet about whom Moses wrote. Their assessment of Jesus as the Prophet is not wrong; however, we know it is a limited realization because Jesus is more than just a prophet. Jesus even spoke of Himself in comparison to Moses in 5:46–47. It is reasonable to believe that some of the multitudes had heard the discourse of Jesus after healing the man at the pool of Bethesda.

The faith of the multitude is based upon signs, and Jesus's response in verse 15 suggests that sign faith can be misdirected for improper motives. John implies the omniscience (all-knowingness) of Jesus in that He perceives their intentions to forcibly make Him a king, even though they label Him the Prophet. This feeding miracle could have been fertilizer for the Zealots, a militant movement seeking the nationalistic brand of Judaism.[230] John's writing in 6:15 informs the reader why Jesus would not be manipulated by the desires of the multitude and His immediate action to distance Himself and the disciples from them. The Synoptic writings do not give Jesus's reason for leaving but simply inform us of Jesus's and the disciples' departure.

In terms of the impact of this miracle on the crowd, they show progression to a level of sign faith that was motivated by human ambition. Of course, we know that sign faith is better than no faith at all; however, it is not equivalent to saving faith, which is dependent upon knowing the identity of Jesus Christ, Son of God. I believe it is safe to say that the immediate audience did not fully grasp the identity of Jesus. Let us now consider the impact of this feeding miracle on the church.

---

[229] Moloney, 198.

[230] Kostenberger, *John*, 203.

Impact of the Miracle on the Church
(Early and Present-Day)

The impact of feeding the five thousand has generated numerous opinions and theories regarding the bread, the fish, and the interpretation of these elements. I will not address the plethora of theories but merely highlight a few common opinions regarding this miracle sign.

Samuel Kobia states, "The feeding of the five thousand is a miracle of sharing and of caring for each other. Seeing the contribution of the five loaves and two fish by the young boy, the community took out the food each of them was carrying. And a fiesta was prepared!"[231] In essence, Kobia argues that the miracle was not the multiplying of the bread and fish but rather a shaming of the multitude to the point of sharing food they had in their possession. I struggle with this theory because it strikes at the core of the miraculous sign pointing to the identity of Jesus.

1) Nothing in the text of John's gospel or the Synoptics suggests the multitude was carrying food, let alone willing to share it one with another.

2) Kobia's theory removes the supernatural intervention of a deity and places this feeding narrative within humanity's capacity to satisfy the expectations of the multitude. It is also difficult to explain the multitude's motivation for sharing to everyone's satisfaction and then provide a surplus of twelve baskets of fragments. John does not inform the reader of any persuading words of Jesus that would have prompted this type of food sharing. The attitude of the disciple Philip (6:7) and those disciples in the Synoptic writing (Matt.

---

[231] Samuel Kobia, "What's in a Miracle? Feeding the Five Thousand," *The Ecumenical Review* 59, no. 4 (October 2007): 534.

14:15; Mark 6:35–37; Luke 9:12) would suggest they were not in a sharing mood.

3) The recognition of the sign by the men in 6:14 and their statement about Jesus being the Prophet does not make sense with Kobia's theory of a miracle of sharing. Carson argues that the fourth gospel writer is portraying this as a miracle and not an ethical lesson of people sharing their lunches.[232] I see no reason to accept this lunch-sharing theory in place of a miraculous sign performed by Jesus.

Brown, Moloney, and O'Day are theologians who support the interpretation of the feeding of the five thousand as being symbolic of the Eucharist, "a sacrament and the central act of worship in many Christian churches, in which bread and wine are consecrated and consumed in remembrance of Jesus' death."[233] In other words, the miracle of the feeding of the five thousand reminds the reader of the Lord's Supper that is administered periodically in many Christian churches.

Brown suggests that "the feeding reminds the reader of the eucharist and the eucharisteo = to give thanks."[234] Brown is not alone, as Moloney suggests that this miracle of breaking bread, distributing it, and gathering fragments tend to blend "the Passover tradition with the Christian tradition that surrounds the ongoing celebration of the Eucharist."[235] John tells us that this miracle occurs during the Passover season, which further links this narrative to the period in which the Lord gave the children of Israel manna from heaven. Moloney also implies that the wilderness gathering of manna is symbolic of the gathering of fragments. The fragment gathering

---

[232] Carson, 270.

[233] *The American Heritage College Dictionary*, 3rd ed., s. v. "Eucharist."

[234] Brown, *The Gospel and Epistles of John*, 42.

[235] Moloney, 198.

can be symbolic of Jesus in that nothing should be lost or wasted.[236] Perhaps a note of caution could be given here to remind the current-day church to beware of how we handle the sacraments, and proclaim the Bread of Life.

O'Day and Hylen offers support of the Eucharist by writing that the feeding miracle described in

> John 6 contributes to contemporary understanding of the Eucharist, especially for Protestant churches that reserve the celebration of the Eucharist for special days or think it is only as a mark of the death of Jesus. The discourse in John 6 is the place where institution of the Eucharist is lodged, because for John, all of Jesus' life institutes the sacrament of the Eucharist, not one particular event at the end of Jesus' life.[237]

I'm afraid I have to disagree with Brown, Moloney, and O'Day regarding the miracle of feeding the five thousand with broken bread and fish being John's way of inserting the Eucharist celebration. For the most part, the Eucharist is not a "eat until you are satisfied" type of celebration but rather a small token of bread and wine that represents the body and blood of our Lord Jesus Christ. The volume of food and leftovers is problematic in comparing this miraculous feeding to the Lord's Supper. I believe we would be on more solid ground to advocate that the bread and fish are symbolic of a person instead of a sacrament. Utley supports my position:

> The Gospel of John does not record the Lord's Supper itself, although chapters 13–17 record the dialogue and prayer in the Upper Room. This omission may be intentional. The church of the second century began to view the ordinances in a sacramental sense. They saw them as channels of grace.

---

[236] Ibid.

[237] O'Day and Hylen, 79.

John may have been reacting to the sacramental view by not recording Jesus' baptism or the Lord's Supper.[238]

When considering the religious climate of that period in history, we must be careful not to assume that John had a Eucharistic view of feeding the five thousand. Utley also informs us that "the early church fathers did not all agree that this passage refers to the Lord's Supper. Clement of Alexandria, Origen and Eusebius never mention the Lord's Supper in their discussions on this passage."[239] This feeding narrative is an indicator of the identity of Jesus as the Son of God as opposed to the Lord's Supper.

The discourse in John 6:22–71 informs the reader that Jesus is "the bread of life" (6:35, 48, 51). Jesus demonstrates His creativeness in multiplying the bread and fish after giving thanks, and then He explains Himself as the metaphor for bread in the discourse the next day (6:22ff). The physical bread multiplied represents the spiritual bread that can only be ascertained by hearing and receiving the truth of His being the One sent from God. Therefore, I would argue that the impact of this feeding narrative on the church today is to show Jesus as the source of life (1:4).

Ashley contends that God's actions were demonstrated in the Passover Feast in the past, and now His actions would be shown by giving His Son as the sacrificial lamb.[240] While the disciples did not grasp the full meaning of the discourse in John 6:22–71, Ashby argues that John's objective in inserting this narrative was "to record Jesus' teaching that He is the life-giving sacrifice bringing liberation and life to all who accept him as such."[241] Richardson agrees with Ashby:

---

[238] Utley, 58.

[239] Ibid.

[240] Godfrey William Ashby, "Body and Blood in John 6:41–65," *Neotestamentica* 36, no. 1–2 (2002): 59.

[241] Ibid., 59.

The Feeding Miracles are clearly to be understood as prophetic actions pointing forward to that moment when the Son of Man was to give his body for the life of the world, the Christian paschal Lamb. The Fourth Evangelist underlines this truth by pointedly stating that the miracle of the Five Thousand took place at Passover-time (John 6:4).[242]

The current-day church seems to focus on the meaning of the bread; however, the fish was equally important for the early church. Myers informs us,

> The sign of the fish was used by the early Church as a secret Christian insignia as well as a symbol representing Christ and the Eucharist in art and literature. This symbol may derive from an appellation for the disciples, "fishers of men" (Luke 5:10), or from Jesus' miraculous feeding of the five thousand (Matt. 14:13–21 par.). The word is an acronym whose letters represent I(ēsous) Ch (ristos) Th (eou) Y (ios) S (ōtēr), meaning Jesus Christ, Son of God, Savior.[243]

Weber supports the importance of fish in the feeding narrative as playing

> an important part in early Christian Eucharistic symbolism. Bread and fish appear frequently in early Christian frescoes in the catacombs as symbols of the Eucharist, and in St. Luke 24:42 f. and John 21:1–14, the Risen Lord, the host at the Eucharist, is associated with the symbolism of the fish.[244]

---

[242] Alan Richardson, "The Feeding of the Five Thousand Mark 6:34–44," *Interpretation* 9, no. 2 (Apr 1955): 144–149.

[243] Myers, *The Eerdmans Bible Dictionary* (Grand Rapids, MI: Eerdmans, 1987), 512.

[244] S. K. Weber, *Matthew* Vol. 1 (Nashville: Broadman and Holman Publishers, 2000), 147.

Farrer suggests that "the fish in the Feeding Miracle are analogous to the quails, as the bread is analogous to the manna, in Moses's miracle of Exodus 16 and Numbers 11."[245]

My research of the impact of this feeding narrative on the latter church seems by and large a split among various theories: the Eucharist activities adhered to in today's church, Jesus as the Passover Lamb (1 Cor. 5:7), and Jesus as the Bread (6:35) who offers life to those who have faith in Him. We will move now to whether this sign gives sufficient reason to believe that Jesus is the Son of God.

Whether This Sign Gives Sufficient Reason to Believe Jesus Is the Son of God

This miraculous sign of the feeding of the five thousand gives sufficient reason to believe that Jesus is the Son of God, and I believe there are several reasons to support this opinion.

(1) The men's reaction and their perception of Jesus (6:13–14) is one source of support. John reveals the belief of the men in 6:14. Moloney says that "they were looking for a figure who would satisfy their expectations—Jesus like a Moses-like prophet from the wilderness days."[246] John also gives insight in 6:15 of the motives of these men perceived by Jesus that they intended to make Him their king forcibly. Clearly, from these men's perception of Jesus, they realized something very special about Jesus. Culpepper states, "They perceive correctly that Jesus is a king, but do not recognize the nature of his kingship, a topic to which the gospel returns in the trial before Pilate (John 18:33–38)."[247] The

---

[245] Austin Farrer, *A Study in St. Mark* (Westminster: Dacre Press, 1951), 291.
[246] Moloney, 198.
[247] Culpepper, "Cognition in John," 251–260.

audience's reaction was based upon more than a meal of sharing food; it was a meal provided by Jesus whereby five barley loaves of bread and two small fish were multiplied and satisfied the multitude with twelve baskets of fragments remaining.

(2) John's inclusion of this feeding narrative collaborates nicely with the Synoptic Gospels in adding validity to the miraculous sign. The narrative details in all of these Gospels are relatively the same, with some minor differences. I suspect that John wanted to show the likeness to God of His Son Jesus (1:1) as a Creator and provider for the physical and spiritual needs of the people. Jesus was able to abundantly satisfy the physical hunger of the multitude and meet the spiritual need, in that He is the Bread of Life (6:35) offered to those willing to accept Him. While some opinions of this narrative claim it is Eucharistic or even suggest correctly that the Passover season hints at Jesus as the Passover lamb, I believe the discourse following the feeding narrative in John 6 unmistakably points us to the identity of Jesus as the Son of God. It is the revelation of Jesus that John wants the reader to grasp from this miraculous sign. For this reason, I believe John includes it as supports in the gospel's purpose expressed in 20:31. Let us now move to the passage of Jesus walking on the sea.

CHAPTER 7

Jesus Walks on Water

Background Information

John introduces the narrative of Jesus walking on the sea as he sets the background scene where this miraculous sign occurs. Jesus has departed into the mountains (6:15), and the disciples have been sent across the sea toward Capernaum (6:16). The body of water John refers to in 6:16 is the Sea of Galilee, sometimes called the Sea of Tiberias (6:1). Ryan informs us that "Tiberias is mentioned by name only three times in the New Testament, and all three references come from the Gospel of John (John 6:1, 23; 21:1). Of those references, two (6:1; 21:1) refer to the 'Sea of Tiberias,' apparently a synonym for the Sea of Galilee."[248] Our writer John references in 6:23 that "other boats came from Tiberias"; however, it is interesting that none of the Gospels show Jesus ministering in Tiberias.[249]

---

[248] J. Ryan, "Tiberias," in *The Lexham Bible Dictionary,* eds. J. D. Barry, D. Bomar, D. R. Brown, R. Klippenstein, D. Mangum, C. Sinclair Wolcott, … W. Widder, (Bellingham, WA: Lexham Press, 2016).

[249] Ibid.

The disciples were en route across the sea to Capernaum, considered a primary location of Jesus's earthly ministry. Capernaum was a bustling fishing center (Matt. 4:18–22) where Peter, Andrew, James, John, and Matthew were called to be Jesus's disciples.[250] Our writer does not tell us why the disciples were on their way to Capernaum; however, we know that Peter lived in Capernaum (Matt. 8:14), and perhaps they were going to his home.

The Sea of Galilee was characterized by "sudden and violent storms (Mt. 8:23–27; Mk. 4:35–41; Lk. 8:22–25), caused by the collision of the warm and cold air."[251] Moloney supports this assessment by stating that "the eastern coast of the normally placid Sea of Galilee is formed by high country split by deep gorges. Sudden changes of weather can tunnel strong winds through the gorges and create difficult conditions on the lake."[252] The natural environment of the Sea of Galilee was frequent turbulence, which fueled the ideology of the sea as a place of chaos in Hebrew literature.[253] O'Day and Hylen articulate, "Water is traditionally a symbol of chaos, over which God alone has power. When Jesus walks on the sea, it becomes apparent that He, like God, can calm the chaos of the sea."[254] John emphasizes the sea and its condition to impress upon the reader the magnitude of the miraculous sign that Jesus will perform.

The fourth gospel author provides the distance of the miracle setting as being "three or four miles" from the previous shore where they entered the boat (6:19). Newman says, *"three or four miles* (so also *Mft*, RSV, JB, *NEB*) is literally 'twenty-five or thirty stadia.' A 'stadium' was about 607 feet. In languages where the metric system is better known, this distance may be expressed as 'five or six

---

[250] Winstead, "Capernaum," *The Lexham Bible Dictionary*, 2016.

[251] Elwell and Beitzel, "Galilee, Sea of," *Baker Encyclopedia of the Bible*, Vol. 1 (Grand Rapids, MI: Baker Book House, 1988), 837.

[252] Moloney, 198.

[253] Culpepper, *The Gospel and Letters of John*, 157.

[254] O'Day and Hylen, 73.

kilometers.'"[255] The distance on the sea should refute any attempts to suggest that Jesus was walking on the shore when the disciples saw Him. Borchert also agrees that the theory of Jesus walking along the shore and the disciples' boat being close to the shore completely refuses to recognize the divine-human events of the story.[256] Let us now consider the characters involved in this miracle sign.

Characters Involved in the Miracle

John's writing does not identify the disciples' names, and we will not spend a lot of time speculating on the number of disciples or their names. We will, however, mention that Philip and Andrew were involved in the conversation with Jesus before the miraculous sign of feeding the five thousand (6:7–8). In Matthew's passage about Jesus' walking on the sea (14:28), Peter is challenged with walking on water; it is reasonable to assume that at least Philip, Andrew, and Peter were among the disciples in the boat. Collectively the disciples are characterized as being afraid when they see Jesus walking on the sea. Matthew and Mark give the reason for their fear: they believed they saw a ghost (14:26, 4:49). John does not give the reason for the disciples' fear, but he does inform the reader that they recognized Jesus. Perhaps John is more interested in Jesus's walking on the sea instead of explaining the disciples' fear.[257]

Jesus is naturally the primary character involved in this miraculous sign. Sherri Brown tells us, "In the Gospel of John, Jesus' power over the waters identifies him with God, and the water imagery in his teaching affirms the provocative nature of his

[255] B. M. Newman and E. A. Nida, *A Handbook on the Gospel of John* (New York: United Bible Societies, 1993), 186.

[256] Borchert, 259.

[257] Carson, 275.

messianic mission."[258] It is a revelation of the true nature of God through His Son, Jesus Christ, in showing His power over water and the forces of nature. Jesus demonstrates His God-like attributes in that He sent the disciples across the sea; rough waters confront them, and then Jesus comes to them during their crisis. Let us look closer at the miraculous sign of Jesus's walking on the sea.

Explanation of the Miracle: Power over Natural Laws

John gives us a narrator's view of the scene by informing us that Jesus's disciples entered the boat in the evening and proceeded to cross the sea without Jesus abroad. He further sets the scene by telling us that it was dark in the evening, a great wind was blowing, and the disciples had rowed only about three or four miles. We can add to the magnitude of this miracle by injecting comments from Matthew's gospel about the boat being "in the middle of the sea and tossed by the waves" (14:24). Mark's writing also tells us of the "straining at rowing, for the wind was against them" (6:48). The stormy weather conditions on the sea help set the stage for a theophany (an appearance of a god to a human being) when these disciples saw Jesus walking on the sea (6:19). Whereas Matthew (14:26) and Mark (6:49) indicate that the disciples thought it was a ghost, John simply tells us that the disciples were afraid. O'Day and Hylen support this position by stating that "John's language suggests that the disciples experience a theophany; they see Jesus as God."[259]

The camouflage of darkness and the rough sea potentially limited the disciples' ability to see Jesus and remain in control of their fears. Jesus's response is appropriate given the disciples' situation. Jesus responds to their fear by telling them, "It is I; do not be afraid"

---

[258] Sherri Brown, "Water Imagery and the Power and Presence of God in the Gospel of John," *Theology Today*, Vol. 72 (2015): 290.

[259] O'Day and Hylen, *John*, 73.

(6:20). O'Day and Hylen comments, "The words 'do not be afraid,' are a response to the disciples' fear and also echo words appropriate to a close encounter with God. (See Gen. 15:1; 26:24; Dan. 10:12, 19; Matt. 28:5; Luke 1:3, 30; 2:10; Acts 27:24; Rev. 1:17)."[260] Culpepper suggests that Jesus's response helped the disciples recognize Him since He was doing "something that in the Hebrew scriptures God alone could do (Job 9:8; Ps 77:16, 19; 107:23–30)."[261] Borchert explains,

> In the present story, the words are *egō eimi* ("I am"). Many have debated whether the *egō eimi* here is merely a self-identification statement, "It is I" (cf. NIV 6:20). The reason for the present review of the theophany pattern is to suggest that the identification cannot be other than a divine identification statement. Moreover, given the use of "I am" (*egō eimi*) throughout this Gospel, it seems to me that the connection with the identification of God's name at Exodus 3:14 argues strongly for "I am."[262]

It is easy to follow the concept of these words pointing us to the divine identification of Jesus since it would tie in nicely with John's purpose; however, there are questionable opinions. Michaels has a different assessment of the response of Jesus.

> Jesus has used the expression, "It is I" once before in our Gospel, identifying himself to the Samaritan woman as the Messiah she was expecting (4:26). Here he is not making a Christological statement, but simply reassuring his disciple by identifying himself as someone known to them, their

---

[260] Ibid.
[261] Culpepper, "Cognition in John," 251–260.
[262] Borchert, 259.

Teacher (see 1:38), who had been with them on the mountain (v. 3), and had stayed on there alone (v. 15).[263]

Carson also agrees with Michaels that the expression "It is I" is ordinary language and does not necessarily convey a theological message, especially since these same words are used by the man born blind (9:9).[264] Carson does, however, concede that the writer of John could be introducing dialogue to point the reader toward grasping the revelation of Jesus Christ, which is the purpose of the gospel writing.[265]

John concludes this narrative with a willingness of the disciples to receive Jesus into the boat, and then immediately the boat was at the shore (6:21). Understandably, the disciples would receive Jesus into the boat; after all, He is their teacher. What bears the implication of a second miracle is the fact that "immediately the boat was at the land where they were going" (6:21). Gangel suggests that we should "not move too quickly over the word 'immediately' in verse 21. With little fuss and no intent to make a point, John probably indicated another miracle which few count in numbering the miracles in John."[266] The Synoptic writers Matthew and Mark are silent regarding the speed with which the boat reached land. So, whether the remainder of the voyage to land was swift or Jesus simply performed another miracle in transporting the boat to shore remains a debatable discussion for further research. We will move to examine other miracles similar to Jesus's walking on water.

---

[263] Michaels, 357.
[264] Carson, 275.
[265] Ibid., 276.
[266] Gangel, 121.

Other Miracles Similar to Jesus's Walking on Water

I want to advocate from the outset that the narrative of Jesus walking on the sea is unique and stands alone regarding a miraculous sign of the deity of Jesus Christ. Matthew's gospel records an incident in 14:28–30 of Peter walking on the sea at the invitation command of Jesus. However, Peter's walk is brief compared to Jesus's, and it ends in Peter's rescue by Jesus, who is still on the water (14:31). I am not aware of any other biblical accounts of individuals walking on water.

Greco-Roman mythology has stories of individuals and objects traveling over water at high speeds; however, these are not like our narrative of Jesus. McPhee states,

> There are numerous examples—far more than have been recognized—of running, chariot-riding, and flying over water beginning as early as Homer's Iliad. Whereas Jesus's feat is presented as a sort of levitation miracle, water running, and water riding are understood as a consequence of superhuman speed in the popular Greek conception of physics, with the idea ultimately based on the motion of wind over waves. Flying over water and other surfaces is associated in Greek thought with super-natural travel convenience; requires speed and flying devices that are entirely foreign to the Gospel narratives. As with water runners, the consistent emphasis on the speed of those who fly over water stands in marked contrast to Jesus's slow walking (περιπατέω).[267]

John's writing and the Synoptic Gospels of Matthew and Mark do not state or imply that Jesus moved at a high rate of speed over the water. All of the Gospels state that Jesus was walking on the sea instead of running (Matt. 14:26; Mark 6:48–49; John 6:19).

---

[267] McPhee, 763–777.

I suspect John's reason for inserting this miraculous sign was to show that the disciples experienced a theophany as often described in the Old Testament teaching of God's power to reveal Himself to humankind and control the sea (Gen. 15:1, 26:24, 46:3; Exodus 14; Ps. 29:3, 65:7, 89:9). Perhaps John even attempts to play on the divine nature of Jesus as God (John 1:1) and cause the reader to reflect on Genesis 1:2b: "And the Spirit of God was hovering over the face of the waters." The only one capable of walking on water in the manner in which Jesus did is God Himself. I believe that is the essence of this miraculous sign. Let us now consider the impact of this miracle on the disciples.

Impact of the Miracle on the Disciples

The impact of this miracle on the disciples will be addressed from the narrative in John's gospel with insight from the accounts in Matthew's and Mark's gospel. In John's writing, he informs the reader in 6:19 that the disciples "saw Jesus walking on the sea" and later, in 6:21, "willingly received Him into the boat." This action by the disciples would be normal considering the weather conditions and probably at face value would imply that they knew Jesus as their master. Culpepper contends, "There is no explicit statement of recognition. Instead, the recognition is implied in the disciples' response, wanting to take Jesus into the boat, a physical reunion."[268] I would agree with Culpepper to some extent; however, it is reasonable to speculate that the disciples' faith was strengthened by seeing Jesus's walk on the sea when we consider future events.

John's writing suggests more than mere recognition by the disciples in 6:68–69 when Peter states, "Lord, to whom shall we go? You have the words of eternal life. Also, we have come to believe and know that You are the Christ, the Son of the living God." Hughes

---

[268] Culpepper, "Cognition in John," 251–260.

argues that the night's crisis of struggling on the sea, combined with Jesus's coming to them amid their discouragement by walking on water and ministering to their fears, made the difference in Peter's faith.[269] I would support Hughes's position and add that it was probably not just the discourse on the Bread of Life that prompted Peter's response to Jesus's question, "Do you also want to go away?" (6:67) but the previous night of struggling on the sea and seeing Jesus walk on it.

When we examine the similar passages in Matthew and Mark, we get a fuller picture of the impact of this miracle on the disciples. Mark tells us that the disciples were "greatly amazed in themselves beyond measure, and marveled" (6:51). While Matthew reveals that "those who were in the boat came and worshipped Him, saying, Truly You are the Son of God" (14:33). Both Matthew and Mark provide a more explicit reaction of the disciples as opposed to John; however, the willing acceptance of Jesus into the boat suggests theological and Christological ideas. Kysar agrees and cautions us that while Matthew's account provides a confession of faith and Mark's account gives a reaction of astonishment, John's insertion of the disciples' welcoming Jesus to enter the boat should not be overlooked.[270]

McReynolds reminds us that Mark's gospel (6:52) adds a comment about the disciples' lack of understanding of the loaves and the hardness of their hearts, which implies that they missed the point of the identity of Jesus.[271] Nevertheless, the intent of John's gospel seems to be focused on showing the reader the identity of Jesus Christ, the Son of God, regardless of the immediate impact of the miracle on the spectators or participators. Let us now move our discussion to the impact on the church regarding the miraculous sign of Jesus's walking on the sea.

---

[269] Hughes, 194.

[270] R. Kysar, *Preaching John* (Minneapolis: Fortress Press, 2002), 187.

[271] P. R. McReynolds, *Mark: Unlocking the Scriptures for You* (Cincinnati: Standard, 1989), 68.

Impact of the Miracle on the Church (Early and Present-Day)

The impact of the miracle of Jesus's walking on the sea has inspired numerous opinions, specifically around the theological application to the church and believers' lives. Hahn suggests that "the close connection between the feeding miracle and the miracle of walking on the sea suggests that the early church saw a theological significance to this miracle.[272] Matthew, Mark, and John all record the narrative of Jesus's walking on the sea, and each of them gives different but nonconflicting reactions from the disciples. The disciples' reaction to the miracle is the worship of Jesus in Matthew (14:33), astonishment in Mark (6:51), and they are welcoming Him aboard in John (6:21). These reactions do not contradict one another but support my opinion that these disciples recognized something unique about Jesus.

Moloney goes on to say, particularly in John's gospel, that "the miracle of the multiplication of loaves and fish did not enhance the crowds' understanding of Jesus. Jesus now gives self-revelation to the disciples, and they receive Him."[273] Hahn comments that Matthew's narrative "is not that readers should respond in awestruck wonder. Rather, *worship* is the point and the appropriate response to this miracle."[274] Rosscup states, "Mark 6:52 does not contradict the faith that Matthew claims the disciples come to here. Astonishment from this new evidence now at sea was a needed jolt, for they had not let former proof of Jesus being the Messiah sink in as they are doing now."[275] In respect to a theological position, the church does not view

---

[272] R. L. Hahn, *Matthew: A Commentary for Bible Students* (Indianapolis: Wesleyan Publishing House, 2007), 186.

[273] Moloney, 198.

[274] Hahn, 186.

[275] J. E. Rosscup, *An Exposition on Prayer in the Bible: Igniting the Fuel to Flame Our Communication with God* (Bellingham, WA: Lexham Press, 2008), 1536.

the disciples' reaction as contradicting the focus of the narrative that is the revelation of Jesus Christ, Son of God, and accepting Him by faith.

The application of this miraculous sign to the church reminds us that crises and circumstances will occur, but we can be encouraged by the power of Jesus over nature. Elowsky makes a couple of comments on John's miracle narrative: (1) the disciples illustrate the dangers of trying to live in this present world without Jesus on board, and (2) the disciples represent the church trying to carry out the mandate of Jesus Christ after His ascension to heaven.[276] In either of Elowsky's comments, the point is that the present-day church is dependent on the divine power of Jesus to overcome the crises it faces.

Brown views the narrative conclusion as an impact on the church to encourage potential disciples to willingly accept Jesus into their hearts as the disciples received Jesus on board the boat (6:1).[277] It raises the issue for today's church to ensure that people voluntarily accept Jesus Christ instead of manipulation or compulsion. The writer John has already introduced in (1:12) the concepts of "receiving" and "believing," and now he illustrates the disciples' reception of Jesus in the boat to support his purpose in writing (20:31). In essence, Brown is suggesting that "in his telling of Jesus and his power over the waters, what John is revealing is the true nature of Jesus and his potential presence in the lives of believers."[278] The precious presence of Jesus is a critical element of the faith within the early and later church. The guarantee of His presence echoes in Scriptures such as Matthew 28:20 and John 14:18, and especially in the promise of the indwelling Holy Spirit in John 14:16. Let us now consider whether the miraculous sign of Jesus's walking on water provides sufficient proof of the deity of Jesus Christ.

---

[276] Elowsky, 219.

[277] Brown, "Water Imagery," 298.

[278] Brown, 298.

Whether This Sign Gives Sufficient Reason to Believe Jesus Is the Son of God

This miraculous sign of Jesus's walking on the sea gives sufficient reason to believe that Jesus is the Son of God, and I believe there are several reasons to support this opinion.

1) The uniqueness of Jesus's walking on the sea identifies Him as the incarnated Word about whom John wrote in 1:1–3 and 14. Culpepper notes that this miracle demonstrates the sovereignty of Jesus as the creative Logo incarnate.[279] John's gospel does not include the sea's rough weather conditions as the passages in Matthew (14:24) and Mark (6:48) do, but he does include the wind blowing. In essence, John portrays Jesus's power over the sea in that He walks on it and His supremacy over the wind in that He is not affected by it. Knowles advocates that "Jesus shows that he is the Lord of the winds and waves. He enacts the words of Psalm 107:30."[280] I like Psalm 107:29–30, which reads, "He calms the storm so that its waves are still. Then they are glad because they are quiet; so He guides them to their desired haven." Jesus illustrates this psalm and shows His divine lordship by walking on the sea and bringing the disciples immediately to shore.

2) The identification of Jesus while walking on the sea has been debated by many scholars. I am aware that Carson argues that the expression *egō eimi* (lit. "I am") carries no theological baggage and is a normal way to say "It is I" in response to the disciples' fear.[281] I am also mindful of Michaels's position that Jesus is simply assuring His

---

[279] Culpepper, *The Gospel and Letters of John*, 157.
[280] Knowles, 512.
[281] Carson, 275.

disciples of who He is instead of making a Christological statement of Himself.[282] However, I find this inclusion of *egō eimi* in this narrative in John to be more than just a mere response to the disciples' fear. I tend to agree with Borchert that the use of "I am" *(egō eimi)* in other parts of the gospel tends to connect the identification of God's name recorded in Exodus 3:14.[283] It is difficult to accept that John would insert these exact words of Jesus as an identifier of Himself to the disciples without realizing that his reader would draw the connection to his purpose in 20:31. Lincoln states that Jesus "is being presented as the embodiment of the God who walks on the water and whose self-proclamation is 'I Am; do not be afraid.'"[284] I agree with Lincoln's opinion and believe there is sufficient evidence to validate the deity of Jesus Christ, the Son of God.

---

[282] Michaels, 357.

[283] Borchert, 259.

[284] A. T. Lincoln, *The Gospel According to Saint John* (London: Continuum, 2005), 218–219.

CHAPTER 8

Jesus Heals the Man Born Blind

Background Information

There appears to be an obvious connection between John chapter 8 and John chapter 9. In John 8:59, Jesus leaves the temple after the Jews had attempted to stone Him for saying, "Most assuredly, I say to you, before Abraham was, I AM." These words stirred murderous hostility toward Jesus, but His hour had not come yet. As He departed the temple, John states, "and so passed by" (8:59d); he begins 9:1 with "now as Jesus passed by," in essence continuing the line of thought from the previous chapter.

We can, however, agree with Carson regarding the general proximity of the miracle's location—that Jesus is in Jerusalem, and it probably occurred sometime between the Feast of Tabernacles and the Feast of Dedication.[285] The fact that Jesus encounters the blind

---

[285] Carson, 361.

man as He passes by suggests that the blind man is not in the temple since he would be considered unclean according to Levitical laws.[286]

The pool of Siloam referred to in the Old Testament books of Isaiah 8:6 and Nehemiah 3:15 "was situated within the city walls, at the southern extremity of the Tyropoean valley. It was from Siloam that the water used in the libations at the feast of Tabernacles was drawn."[287] Furthermore, archaeologists are very confident of the location of Siloam in Jerusalem since it was "excavated in 1880, revealing an inscription enabling its identification (Michaels 1983: 150)."[288] The writer John informs the readers in 9:7 that the man born blind was sent to "wash in the pool of Siloam (which is by interpretations, Sent)." Michaels suggests that the water (represent being "Sent") is like unto the Holy Spirit. In essence, the man was similar to a Jew converting to Christianity.[289] Brown argues that there is a possible connection between baptism and the anointing of the blind man's eyes because of Tertullian, St. Augustine, and early catacombs' art showing the healing of the blind man as a symbol of baptism and light healing.[290] I doubt John intended to make a connection between the anointing of the blind man's eyes and baptism. Let us now proceed to the characters, directly and indirectly, involved in the miracle sign.

---

[286] A. Edersheim, *The Temple, Its Ministry and Services as They Were at the Time of Jesus Christ* (London: James Clarke and Co., 1959), 198.

[287] C. K. Barrett, *The Gospel According to John: An Introduction with Commentary and Notes on the Greek Text* (Philadelphia: The Westminster Press, 1978), 358.

[288] Craig Blomberg, *The Historical Reliability of John's Gospel: Issues and Commentary* (Downers Grove Illinois: Inter Varsity Press, 2001), 152.

[289] J. Ramsey Michaels and W. Ward Gasque, *John: New International Commentary* (Peabody, MA: Hendrickson Publishers, 1989), 162.

[290] Brown, *The Gospel and Epistles of John*, 55.

Characters Involved

John's narrative in 9:1–41 comprises numerous characters and their reactions to sight given to the man born blind. The narrative is silent regarding the identification of the man born blind and his parents. The gospel writer leaves the names unknown, perhaps to focus the reader on the symbolism of their characters instead of specific people in history. Bultmann contends that "the man's blindness is synonymous with being in darkness whereas illumination is only possible through revelation by the Revealer."[291] Michaels and Gasque suggest, "Blindness is an appropriate metaphor for sin, even as the ability to see clearly is one for righteousness (cf., e.g., 11:9–10; 12:35–36; 1 John 2:9–11)."[292] I would conclude that the names are not important to this writer but rather the motifs of "darkness versus light" and "sin versus righteousness." We could even surmise that the man born blind moves from darkness to light whereas his parents remain in darkness.

Jesus is naturally the primary character in this miraculous sign of healing the man born blind. Michaels and Gasque remind us that "Jesus takes the initiative at the beginning to meet the blind man and again after he is expelled from the synagogue. In contrast to the warning given the man healed at the pool of Bethesda, Jesus elicits faith in the blind man."[293] There is no indication in John chapter 9 that this blind man solicits healing from Jesus. Jesus is again demonstrating the divine sovereignty of God to manifest His works through the healing of this man born blind (9:3). Jesus's expression of mercy toward this man merely opens the door for a theological debate on sin and blindness, and of course, it just happened to be on the Sabbath day. Barrett agrees that "the blind man was the theme of

---

[291] Bultmann, 341.
[292] Michaels and Gasque, 173.
[293] Ibid.,170.

a theological debate, but he becomes the object of divine mercy and revelation of who Jesus is."[294]

Jesus's disciples are present during the initial discussion of the man born blind; however, John is silent about whether they are witnesses to the miracle itself or even the discussion after that. The question by the disciples in John 9:2 brings to the forefront what Edersheim calls a Jewish belief:

> That children benefited or suffered according to the spiritual state of their parents was a doctrine current among the Jews. But they also held that an unborn child might contract guilt, since the *Yezer ha-ra*, or evil disposition which was present from its earliest formation, might even then be called into activity by outward circumstances. And sickness was regarded as alike the punishment for sin and its atonement.[295]

Moloney also adds that "the disciples' question is based upon a Biblical principle—Num. 14:18; Deut. 5:9."[296] The manifestation of sin in the lives of children and grandchildren is what we call today generational curses. The disciples' question fits with many questions today regarding who is responsible for the congenital disability. But the question goes deeper in that it suggests the child could sin in the womb before being born. Rabbinical commentaries on Genesis 25:22 regarding Esau and Jacob struggling in the womb of Rebekah suggest the potential misconduct of babies before birth. Psalm 58:3 indicates the waywardness and lies of babies at birth, and this scriptural passage refers to Esau's sinful behavior.[297] An unborn child sinning in the womb is challenging to comprehend; however, the

---

[294] Barrett, 358.
[295] Edersheim, *Sketches of Jewish Social Life in the Days of Christ,* 162–163.
[296] Moloney, *The Gospel of John,* 198.
[297] Carson, 362.

impact of the parents' sins is very believable. Edersheim expresses a Jewish belief:

> Up to thirteen years of age, a child was considered, as it were, part of his father and as suffering for his guilt. More than that, the thoughts of a mother might affect the moral state of her unborn offspring, and the terrible apostasy of one of the greatest Rabbis had, in popular belief, been caused by the sinful delight his mother had taken when passing through an idol-grove (Midr. On Ruth 3:13). Lastly, certain special sins in the parents would result in specific diseases in their offspring, and one is mentioned (Nedar. 20a) as causing blindness in the children.[298]

Jesus must respond to the disciples and perform the miraculous sign against the Jewish thinking that someone is responsible for the man's blindness.

John adds the reference to the blind man's neighbors, who had diverse opinions on the subject, to discuss whether the healed man is the same person as the man born blind (9:8–9). It is often easier to reject a miraculous sign and, in this situation, believe the healed man merely had a resemblance to the man born blind.[299] The neighbors are a part of the miracle verification process, but they are also instruments for the opposition because they usher the healed man to the Pharisees (9:10–13). Keener supports the opinion that these neighbors are indecisive regarding the man's identity, and they escort the man before the Pharisees to show their negative position concerning Jesus.[300] John does not suggest in his narrative that these neighbors ever changed their opinion or recognized Jesus as the light

---

[298] Edersheim, *The Life and Times of Jesus the Messiah*, 598.
[299] Carson, 366.
[300] Keener, 784.

of the world. In other words, they remained in darkness and blind to the truth.

The Pharisees represent the Jewish leaders of the local synagogue and are responsible for judicial opinions. Carson suggests that John inserts for us the neighbors' taking him to the Pharisees to get an explanation or clarification of this healing.[301] The Pharisees launch an investigation that, in turn, exposes the miracle performed on the Sabbath day. Interestingly, the Pharisees are not concerned about the healing of the man born blind but rather preserving the legal tradition of adhering to rest on the Sabbath.[302] John shows the division within the Pharisee ranks concerning a person's breaking the law versus performing a good deed. We will discuss more in the section of the impact of the miracle regarding the Pharisees.

Explanation of the Miracle

Jesus prefaces the miracle of healing the man born blind by moving the focus of the conversation from the cause of the blindness to the purpose of the blindness.[303] When we compare this story with the narrative of the man healed at the pool of Bethesda, we see that Jesus implies a relationship between sin and sickness (5:14). In contrast, in 9:3, He indicates that there is not a relationship in all situations of personal illness.[304] Jesus says in 9:3b–4 that the sightlessness of this man is for the glory of God and that He must illuminate the works of the Father while it is day. Brown argues the symbolism of blindness to sin by advocating that "the man's blindness is illustrative of mankind's sinful state."[305] Because there was no known cure for being born blind, this parallels humankind's

---

[301] Carson, 366–367.

[302] Moloney, 293.

[303] Michaels and Gasque, 159.

[304] Blomberg, 151.

[305] Brown, *The Gospel and Epistles of John*, 55.

sinful state of being born in sin (Ps. 51:5) and existing in darkness apart from the light of Jesus.

After Jesus utters the theological statements in verses 4 and 5, He spits saliva on the ground, makes clay, and then anoints the blind man's eyes (9:6). Afterward, Jesus instructs the man to "go, wash in the pool of Siloam (which is translated, Sent)" (9:7). The man exercises what I would call blind faith and obeys the instructions of Jesus. The writer tells us that the man was obedient and "came back seeing" (9:7b), which implies a miracle of eyesight unique to other biblical and historical accounts.

The gospel of Mark records Jesus using spittle to heal a deaf-mute in 7:33 and then a blind man in 8:23; however, in these occurrences, Jesus did not make clay but spit directly onto the tongue and eyes respectively. Michaels compares this miracle to the creation (Gen. 2:7) in which God took clay from the earth and made man.[306] Culpepper also sees the symbolism of the creation when Jesus made clay and anointed the blind man's eyes.[307] Whether John inserts this activity to remind us of the creative power from Genesis 2:7 is debatable; however, this action does comport with the healing methods known during this period in history.

Michaels tells us that it is not uncommon for ancient healers to use saliva after fasting due to the perceived healing properties.[308] Blomberg adds that "saliva was often thought to have medicinal value in the ancient Mediterranean world."[309] Edersheim also supports the fact that saliva was commonly used as a remedy for eye diseases.[310] Jesus appears to be using a healing method with similar characteristics to those of that time period; however, there are no incidents of correcting blindness from birth. The healing of the

---

[306] Michaels and Gasque, 162.

[307] Culpepper, *The Gospel and Letters of John*, 174.

[308] Michaels and Gasque, 161.

[309] Blomberg, 151.

[310] Edersheim, *The Life and Times of Jesus the Messiah*, 599.

blind, in general, is rare in the miracle stories of antiquity, and there is no parallel for healing congenital blindness.[311]

Jesus sends the man born blind to wash in the pool of Siloam after anointing his eyes with the clay. John inserts the meaning of the pool of Siloam as being "sent," which has scriptural symbolism. There are several viewpoints regarding what the pool of Siloam has in relationship to the man born blind. I want to address the pool first regarding actual water purification and second regarding obedience and acceptance of Jesus.

Keener informs us that "the pool of Siloam was reputed to be especially effective for purification, and many proselytes were reportedly immersed there; even to this day some popularly call the pool the *mikveh* of the high priest Ishmael."[312] The festival of Tabernacles included the renowned ritual of water-drawing from the pool of Siloam because this water was considered holy.[313] The concept of using holy water for purification and healing purposes is not uncommon. In John 5:4, at the pool of Bethesda, the stirring of the water by the angel was believed to heal the first person who went into the water. In 2 Kings 5:10–14, Naaman is told to "go and wash in the Jordan seven times, and your flesh shall be restored to you, and you shall be clean." It was not the Jordan that healed Naaman, nor was it the water of the pool of Siloam that healed the man born blind. The healing and restoration were not in the ritual of washing but rather in the divine power of the One sent from above. Keener states, "Because Jesus sends the man to this pool, it becomes clear that John does not oppose ritual water (e.g., 2:6; 3:25) per se; it is just that the traditional rituals of his Jewish heritage are not efficacious apart from an encounter with Jesus."[314]

---

[311] Blomberg, 151.

[312] Keener, 781.

[313] Ibid., 781–782.

[314] Keener, 782.

There is a symbolic viewpoint comparing the pool of Siloam, which means "sent," with the Christology of Jesus being the sent One from above. In John 9:4, Jesus states, "I must work the works of Him who sent Me while it is day; the night is coming when no one can work." Clearly, Jesus is telling the disciples that He has been "sent" by God. Brown sees a wordplay in that "this pool, bearing a name interpreted as 'Sent,' stands in John for Jesus, who is the one sent by the Father."[315] The symbolic viewpoint of "sent" is further illustrated in John 20:21, in which Jesus commissioned His disciples for ministry work.

The man born blind portrays faith and obedience in Jesus, whom he cannot see, in that "he went and washed, and came back seeing" (9:7). In Isaiah 8:6, the Jews rejected the waters of Shiloah, which flow from the Gihon Spring to the pool of Siloam; here in John's narrative, the blind man accepts the instructions from Jesus to go and wash, whereas later the Jewish leaders will reject Jesus, the sent One.[316] During this period in history, the Jews accepted the water from the pool for water-pouring rites of the Feast of Tabernacles, but they would reject the living water from Jesus (4:10), who came from above. Jesus elaborates further on His relationship with the Father and being the "sent" One in John chapter 10. Let us move now to other miracles similar to Jesus's healing the man born blind.

Other Miracles Similar to Jesus Healing the Man Born Blind

Other miracles are similar to Jesus's healing the man born blind; however, this miraculous sign has a uniqueness that makes it stand out. We want to consider nonbiblical examples before comparing

---

[315] Brown, *The Gospel and Epistles of John*, 55.
[316] Carson, 365.

this miracle to other Synoptic accounts. Barrett noted several similar miracles in his research.

> An instructive parallel to the whole incident is found in Dittenberger, *Syll.* 1173.15–18 (Deissmann, 132). To Valerius Aper, a blind soldier, the god revealed that he should go and take the blood of a white cock, together with honey, and rub them into an eyesalve (cf. the use made of clay and spittle, v. 6) and anoint his eyes three days. And he received his sight and came and gave thanks publicly to the god.[317]

There are obvious differences between this miracle and the healing by Jesus.

1) There is no indication that this soldier was blind from birth and, I would think, probably not since he became a soldier.
2) There was no intermediary involved in the miracle, just the blood of a white cock mixed with other ingredients. Are we to believe the soldier's sight was restored based upon the ingredients?
3) The eyes were anointed for three days versus one for anointing and washing in John's account.
4) This sounds Satanic in methodology, and there is no reason not to believe that the soldier was merely temporarily blind.

Barrett also documents "a well-known story of Vespasian at Alexandria (Tacitus, Historiae IV, 81. Suetonius, Vespasian 7; Dio Cassius LXV, 8)."[318] Elowsky wrote in the Ancient Christian commentary the story of Vespasian, a new emperor who did not have faith in healing but later was persuaded to spit upon the eyes of a blind man and touch the leg of a lame man, with this being a successful

---

[317] Barrett, 353.
[318] Elowsky, 358.

healing before a crowd.[319] This story only appears similar to John's narrative because a blind man received sight from the spittle of an emperor. The emperor did not believe he could heal, and there is no record of the man being born blind. Barrett implies that some magical act was involved, and "the use of spittle was in general accompanied by magical practices (cf. Betz, 150), which made it suspect in Judaism."[320] My conclusion regarding Barrett's incidents of similarity is that they do not compare with John's narrative of Jesus healing the man born blind. Let us consider the Synoptic passages of the healing of blind people.

In the Synoptic Gospels are several accounts of Jesus healing blind individuals. In Matthew 9:27–31 and 20:29–34, Jesus touched the blind person, and they received sight. In Mark 10:46–52 and Luke 18:35–42, Jesus speaks to the blind person, and they receive sight. The power of His touch and spoken word produces the miracle of sight in these accounts. However, these examples of healing blindness do not serve as true parallels to the account in John's gospel. Barrett agrees that "the cure of the blind man has no precise parallel in the Synoptic Gospels (for similar stories cf. Mark 8:22–6; 10:46–52)."[321] I agree with Blomberg that the method Jesus used of mixing saliva with clay and then anointing the blind man (vv. 6–7) is unique to John's gospel.[322] Michaels insists that the story of the man born blind differs from the other blind healing because his restoration of sight is like a new birth.[323] In Mark 8:22–26, Jesus uses spittle and touch to cure the blind man, but again there is no indication that these blind people were born blind or instructed to go and wash. Jesus's healing the man born blind places this miraculous sign in a unique category in terms of pointing us toward the objective of John 20:31. Let us now address the impact of this miracle on the attending audience.

---

[319] Ibid., 285.

[320] Ibid.

[321] Barrett, 354.

[322] Blomberg, 151.

[323] Michaels and Gasque, 160.

Impact of the Miracle on the Attending Audience

Four entities are impacted by the miracle of Jesus's healing of the man born blind: the neighbors, the parents of the man born blind, the Pharisees, and the man born blind.

1) The neighbors are indecisive in confirming the identity of the man born blind until his confirmation, "I am he" (9:8–9). Culpepper argues that the gospel writer inserts the neighbors to confirm the man as previously being the man born blind.[324] The division among the neighbors would suggest how many people saw the blind man but did not notice him. Bultmann takes a different position and contends "that the crowd of witnesses is not used to prove the truth of the story by way of conclusion but forms a prelude to the main narrative."[325] I believe there is truth in both scholars' positions. The neighbors with the testimony of the man previously born blind (9:9) offer verification of the man's healing while at the same time ushering him to the Pharisees for judicial review of the healing act. The miracle impacts the neighbors only to validate the miracle and then prompt a judicial review. There is no reason to suspect that they became believers by faith in Jesus.

2) The parents of the man born blind identify their son as being previously blind. John tells us that the real reason for their answer to the Pharisees was the fear of the Jews and the propensity for anyone to be put out of the synagogue who confessed Jesus as the Christ (9:22). When the parents are asked, "How then does he now see?" (9:19). Keener explains that in actuality, the parents did not know and could only offer secondhand testimony, but their motive makes their

---

[324] Culpepper, *The Gospel and Letters of John*, 174.
[325] Bultmann, 333.

statement appear to be a denial.[326] The explanation that their son "is of age; ask him" (9:23) would imply that he is at least thirteen years old and could have been older.[327] Surely the parents would have known who healed their son; however, they made the conscious decision to yield to the religious and social power structure of that day instead of publicly acknowledging Jesus as the Christ. In essence, the miracle of healing had no impact in prompting them to believe in Jesus as the Son of God.

3) The Pharisees never denied the actual miracle of Jesus's giving sight to a man born blind. Jesus's actions broke rabbinic rules for the Sabbath in that He healed with spittle and kneading the clay.[328] Michaels states,

> Precisely the healing of one's eyes with saliva on the Sabbath was forbidden in the Talmud by some rabbis (Shabbath 108a), though the problem over the Sabbath in this case (cf. vv. 14, 16) seems to have arisen because Jesus kneaded the mud into a ball in performing the miracle (the Mishnah, Shabbath 7.2, list "kneading" among 39 activities prohibited on the Sabbath; cf. 24.3).

The Pharisees focused on the miraculous work done on the Sabbath day. If Jesus did the work, He must be a sinner because a man sent from God would not work on the Sabbath.[329] The Pharisees' line of questions does not deny the miracle performed but rather interrogates the character of the miracle worker. Moloney supports Culpepper's position by contending that "the Pharisees are not interested in the

---

[326] Keener, 788.

[327] Ibid.

[328] Brown, *The Gospel and Epistles of John*, 55.

[329] Culpepper, *The Gospel and Letters of John*, 174

healing of the blind man; but rather on the preservation of the legal tradition. Debate breaks out regarding the origin of Jesus and His relationship with the Father."[330] The Sabbath violation opens the door to the main focus, which is the Christological issue. The Pharisees cannot accept any compromise in the debate with the man previously born blind, specifically about being a disciple of Moses versus a disciple of Jesus. This either-or situation for the Pharisees leads ultimately to the man being cast out (9:34).

Bultmann's comment on 9:34 is that the Pharisees view the man born blind as completely in sin, which is the opposite of what Jesus said in 9:3.[331] Once again, the writer, John, offers the narrator's insight for his readers on the spiritual blindness of the Pharisees versus that of the man previously born blind. Michaels highlights how Jesus contrasts two groups: those like the man born blind who accept Him and those like the Pharisees who demonstrate unbelief. "The blind are not guilty; the guilty ones are those who claim to see. The blind man was cured; the Pharisees, by their stubborn refusal to accept the reality of the power of God, only proved themselves blind."[332] In essence, the Pharisees' reaction to the miracle was to reject Jesus and remain in the darkness of their sin. "The blindness of the Pharisees and scribes is incurable since they deliberately rejected the only cure that exists—Jesus the light of the world."[333]

4) The man born blind reacts as a true sinner taking steps toward believing in Jesus. He shows a radical response to

---

[330] Moloney, 293.

[331] Bultmann, 337.

[332] Michaels and Gasque, 173.

[333] Barrett, 366.

the words of Jesus in that he went, he washed, he came back seeing, and then he became a witness to the identity of Jesus. It is not the contact with the waters of Siloam that invoked healing, but contact with the One sent from God and his acceptance of His words.[334] Brown sees the progression of the blind man's faith as validation that he is a son of Abraham versus the Pharisees, who prove they are children of the devil.[335] I would contend that he is not a model Christian at this point, but there is a definite progression in his faith toward Jesus. As we review John 9:24–34 and notice the previously blind man's responses, we see a "progression of faith in his responses >> 'a man called Jesus' > 'a prophet' and then 'from God.'"[336] His testimony is definitive and personal, and perhaps it spiritually characterizes the rebirth about which Jesus spoke to Nicodemus in John 3.[337] This man's reaction to the miraculous healing was not deterred by the questioning, the verbal abuse, or the ex-communication of the Pharisees (9:34). When found by Jesus (9:35), this previously blind man learns that Jesus is the Son of God, and he worships Him (9:38). I believe John wants his readers to come into the knowledge of who Jesus is and worship Him as the Christ, Son of God.

Impact of the Miracle on the Church (Early and Present-Day)

The miracle of the healing of the man born blind, followed by the interaction with the Pharisees, had a significant impact on

---

[334] Moloney, 293.

[335] Brown, *The Gospel and Epistles of John*, 55.

[336] Ibid., 165.

[337] Ibid., 168.

the early and present-day church. Some theologians believe that this miracle encouraged the rift between followers of Jesus Christ and Judaism. Michaels argues that "this is really Judaism versus Christianity – becoming distinct, and rival entities, as the church begins to define itself over against the synagogue."[338] Kysar elaborates further by contending that the Gospel of John was written for a group of Christian Jews who were separated from the synagogue.

> The textual evidence for such a theory is found in the use of the word *aposynagōgos* ("expelled" or "put out of the synagogue") in 9:22, 12:42, and 16:2. Building on that evidence, scholars have proposed that those Christians who formed the Johannine Christian community were originally Jews, perhaps including some Hellenistic Jews. These Christians were convinced that Jesus was indeed the Messiah but saw no reason to leave the synagogue.[339]

Our objective is not to address the audience John was writing to but rather to suggest that this miracle narrative impacted the division within the Jewish religious system of worship. In John 9:16, there is a difference of opinion regarding the miracle because Jesus performed it on the Sabbath day. Blomberg contends that the division among the Pharisees carried down to contemporaries Shammai and Hillel, whose respective schools argued, first, principles (anyone who breaks the law is a sinner) versus, second, the facts of the case (Jesus had performed a good work).[340] The man previously born blind after his conversation with the Pharisees was cast out (9:34), which fueled the theory of ex-communication for those supportive of Jesus's being the Christ (9:22). Blomberg holds to the view that ex-communication

---

[338] Michaels and Gasque, 167.

[339] Kysar, 24.

[340] Blomberg, 153.

from the synagogues did not occur during this time.[341] I will not address the validity of Blomberg's position. Still, I would encourage readers interested in a more detailed discussion of the types of ex-communication from the synagogues to consult the writings of Alfred Edersheim, such as *The Life and Times of Jesus the Messiah* (Hendrickson Publishers, 1993). For now, we will accept the view that in this particular synagogue, ex-communication existed.

This miracle of healing the man born blind impacts the church from a Christological perspective in that Jesus can get rid of human suffering no matter what the cause is.[342] Barrett states that "on the one hand, he is the giver of benefits to a humanity which apart from him is in a state of complete hopelessness; it was never heard that one should open the eyes of a man born blind (v. 32)."[343] So the opening of the blind man's eyes fits perfectly with John's writing of the work of Christ in that He can give sight to the blind as well as life and salvation to those who believe in Him. The concept of being blind from birth fits compatibly with the concept of being born in sin.

I would agree with scholars that the man born blind is, in essence, a representation of individuals being born in sin. Barrett reminds us in his comments on 9:3 that "John wants the reader to know that the man's birth and blindness are not outside the control and purpose of God."[344] The church's concept of sin is exposed in this narrative. It is not the blind in sin but those who refuse to see when the light of truth is shined upon them. Culpepper says, "Sin lies not in being born blind but in refusing to see when one is confronted with the light."[345] Clearly, this narrative in John's writing shows the Pharisees as representatives of the group that refused to see the light of truth in the miracle performed by Jesus. In essence, they

---

[341] Blomberg, 153–154.

[342] Culpepper, *The Gospel and Letters of John*, 174.

[343] Barrett, 354.

[344] Ibid., 156.

[345] Culpepper, *The Gospel and Letters of John*, 178.

demonstrate for us that "sin consists not in being born unbelieving but in refusing to believe when one has seen the power of God at work."[346] Let us now conclude whether this miraculous sign gives sufficient reason to believe that Jesus is the Son of God.

Whether This Sign Gives Sufficient Reason to Believe Jesus Is the Son of God

I believe this miraculous sign furnishes ample reasons to believe that Jesus is the Son of God, and the following are several explanations for consideration:

1) The uniqueness of Jesus's granting sight to a man born blind cannot truly be compared to any other illustration of a person receiving sight. All attempts to find similar examples of people receiving their sight cannot compare to the fact that this man was born blind and that, based upon faith and obedience in the words of Jesus, he received sight (9:7). The nonbiblical examples of cured blindness discussed in the section "Other miracles similar to Jesus's healing the man born blind" cannot be compared to John's narrative. Even the Synoptic examples, while demonstrating the power of Jesus through the spoken word and His touch, are not equivalent to healing a man born blind.

2) The symbolism of this miracle is filled with the characteristics of God in that Jesus initiates the healing of the man: (a) He saw him in 9:1, (b) He anoints the blind man's eyes in 9:6, (c) He sends him to wash in 9:7, (d) He hears about the man and finds him in 9:35, and (e) He reveals Himself as the Son of God in 9:37. The actions of Jesus expose the divine light of who He is as the Son of God. Remember,

---

[346] Ibid., 179.

Bultmann says that "blindness is synonymous with being in darkness. Illumination is possible through revelation by the Revealer."[347] Brown also supports this view by adding that Jesus is the light of the world, and while darkness will have its hour at the cross, the resurrection will validate the power of Jesus.[348] In essence, the miracle reveals God's unexplainable and unimaginable mercy and grace through His Son Jesus.

3) This miraculous sign satisfies the purpose of John's writing based upon 20:31 in that the man born blind receives not only physical sight but also the spiritual sight of who Jesus is. The man who was previously blind is an example of a person moving from unbelief to faith in Jesus. Michaels argues that the man born blind is presented as a disciple of Jesus in that he hears and obeys the voice of Jesus (10:27) by going to wash in the pool of Siloam.[349] He also advocates that the previously blind man serves as a surrogate of Jesus in his confrontation with the Pharisees (9:15–17, 24–34). The healed man does not compromise in his defense of being healed by Jesus.[350] The man shows unwavering faith in Jesus, whom he had not seen until later found by Jesus (9:35), and fulfills the purpose of 20:31.

---

[347] Bultmann, 341.

[348] Brown, *The Gospel and Epistles of John,* 55.

[349] Michaels and Gasque, 160.

[350] Ibid., 163.

CHAPTER 9

Jesus Raises Lazarus from the Grave

Background Information

In John 10:40, the writer of the fourth gospel informs us that Jesus is located "beyond the Jordan to the place where John was baptizing at first, and there He stayed." According to Elwell and Beitzel, Bethany was the

> village on "the other side of the Jordan" (the east side), where John the Baptist baptized (Jn 1:28). The KJV has "Bethabara," found in many manuscripts and thought correct by the 3rd-century church father Origen, who suggested that Bethabara meant "house of preparation," an appropriate location for John's ministry. The most logical site for this Bethany is the present-day Qasr el-Yehud.[351]

---

[351] Elwell and Beitzel, "Bethany," *Baker Encyclopedia of the Bible*, Vol. 1 (Grand Rapids, MI: Baker Book House, 1988), 285.

It appears that John is trying to avoid confusing his reader and tells us that Jesus is located beyond the Jordan, which is a different place from the Bethany where Lazarus, Martha, and Mary are located. Guyer comments that the "Bethany beyond the Jordan refers to the location of John the Baptist's early ministry and the place where Jesus was baptized (John 1:28)."[352]

I believe John wants the reader to recognize two distinct villages and the distance between them as he sets the storyline for why Jesus does not travel expediently to heal Lazarus. Fullilove states that "the Bethany where Mary, Martha, and Lazarus lived was over 15 miles from the Jordan (Origen, *Commentary on John*, VI 24; Ante Nicene Fathers X, p.370), which seems too far a distance to be described as 'across from the point of the Jordan.'"[353] Newman states that "the *Bethany* referred to here is not the Bethany of 1:28. The Bethany of this verse is identified with the modern town of El' Azariyeh, just east of Jerusalem. The modern name of the town is itself derived from the name Lazarus."[354] It is my opinion that these are different villages with the same name, Bethany.

The Bethany where Lazarus was sick was in a village on the eastern slope of the Mount of Olives between one and two miles east of Jerusalem. This Bethany was close to Bethphage, where Jesus made His triumphal entry to Jerusalem.[355] The same Bethany where Jesus and his disciples sometimes stayed when they attended temple observances during Passover (Matt. 21:17; Mark 11:11)[356] and when "Jesus was eating at the home of Simon the leper in Bethany

---

[352] M. S. Guyer, "Bethany on the Mount of Olives," *The Lexham Bible Dictionary*, eds. J. D. Barry, D. Bomar, D. R. Brown, R. Klippenstein, D. Mangum, C. Sinclair Wolcott, ... W. Widder, (Bellingham, WA: Lexham Press, 2016).

[353] W. B. Fullilove, "Bethany Beyond the Jordan," in *The Lexham Bible Dictionary*, eds. J. D. Barry, D. Bomar, D. R. Brown, R. Klippenstein, D. Mangum, C. Sinclair Wolcott, ... W. Widder, (Bellingham, WA: Lexham Press, 2016).

[354] Newman and Nida, 354.

[355] Elwell and Beitzel, "Bethany," *Baker Encyclopedia of the Bible*, 284–285.

[356] Ibid.

when a woman came and anointed his head with costly perfume (Mt. 26:6–13; Mk. 14:3–9)."[357] These are two distinct villages about fifteen miles apart, and the location also helps us understand the presence of the Jews in Bethany (9:36–37, 45) due to their proximity to Jerusalem.

Characters Involved

Jesus is the primary character in this miraculous sign, and once again, He is satisfying the will of the Father to bring glory to His name. This narrative of the resurrection of Lazarus appears to conclude the Book of Signs and highlight the motif of "life" based upon 1:4. Latourelle states that "the theme of life is a favorite of John, just as the theme kingdom of heaven is to the Synoptic Gospels. In the Synoptics, life is presented in a future state whereas, in John, Jesus is life and the giver of life."[358] John once again shows the commitment of Jesus to bring glory to the Father (11:4) despite the potential hostility of the Jews (11:8). Essentially, this example of devotion to the Father's will as performed by Jesus is a model for the believer's life.

The writer of the fourth gospel introduces Lazarus as a "certain man" but identifies him as being from "Bethany, the town of Mary and her sister Martha" (11:1). This introduction of Lazarus distinguishes him from the Lazarus in Luke's parable (16:19–31). The Lazarus in Luke's writing is a beggar who lays at the gate and dies, whereas the Lazarus in John's writing lives in Bethany, dies, but is resurrected. The request for Jesus to come to Bethany because "Lord, behold he who You loves is sick" (11:3) further distinguishes this Lazarus from Luke's parable because there is no mention of the close relationship between Luke's Lazarus and Jesus.

---

[357] Ibid.

[358] Rene Latourelle, *The Miracles of Jesus and the Theology of Miracles*, trans. Matthew J. O'Connell (Mahwah, NJ: Paulist Press, 1988), 229.

"*Lazarus* is the Greek form of the Hebrew name Eleazar, which means 'God helps.'"[359] The acting out of Lazarus's name in terms of the help of God is demonstrated in John's gospel telling of the resurrection of Lazarus. In contrast, even the request in Luke 16:19–31 to send Lazarus to warn the rich man's family is denied. While it is true that Jesus loved more than one disciple (11:5), it is very doubtful that Luke's Lazarus and John's Lazarus are the same. It is even further doubtful considering the opinion that John's Lazarus is potentially the disciple whom Jesus loved in 21:20 or possibly the author of the fourth gospel.[360] I believe it is a safer opinion to read the text at face value in viewing this Lazarus in John's writing as the brother of Mary and Martha who lived in the village of Bethany a few miles from Jerusalem.

Mary is distinguished from the mother of Jesus and identified as "that Mary who anointed the Lord with fragrant oil and wiped His feet with her hair, whose brother Lazarus was sick" (11:2). This Mary was probably well known for this act of anointing Jesus.[361] Based upon the prophetic words of Jesus in Matthew 26:13 and Mark 14:9, we are still reading and discussing Mary's action of anointing Jesus. In Luke's writing, she is spiritually receptive and devoted to Jesus as she sits at His feet (10:39), listening to His words. Lockyer distinguishes this Mary in John's writing from the nameless woman in Luke 7:37–37 because the nameless sinner woman anointed Jesus's feet as an expression of gratitude for being forgiven and cleansed.

In contrast, Mary anoints as an expression of gratitude for the resurrection of her brother Lazarus (12:3).[362] Elwell and Beitzel remind us that the nameless woman in Luke's gospel is located in

---

[359] Newman and Nida, 353–354.

[360] Blomberg, 166.

[361] Blomberg, 165.

[362] Herbert Lockyer, R.S.L, *All the Women of the Bible* (Grand Rapids, MI: Zondervan Publishing House), 103.

Galilee, while the Mary in John's gospel is in Judea.[363] There are other women called Mary in the New Testament; however, we will conclude that this Mary in John's narrative has written identifiers (11:1–2).

John identifies Martha as the sister of Mary, living in the town of Bethany. In 11:7, he informs us that "Jesus loved Martha, and her sister, and Lazarus." In Luke 10:38–42, Martha shows hospitality to Jesus and His disciples. MacArthur claims that "Martha seemed to be the elder of the two sisters."[364] Luke 10:38 states that "Martha received him into her house," which implies that Martha possibly owned the house. MacArthur also contends that her house ownership combined "with the fact that her name was usually listed first whenever she was named with her siblings, implies strongly that she was the elder sister."[365] I agree with Michaels that "perhaps Martha is being transformed from a busy woman in Luke 10:38 to a woman of words and faith in John's writing." [366]

The prior verses 7, 8, 12, and 14 do not inform us of how many disciples are present or who was present, other than "Thomas, who is called the Twin," in verse 16. The disciples of Jesus are unidentified until verse 16, in which Thomas boasts of their willingness to go and die with Jesus. These details of the disciples appear to be of little significance to John's purpose in this Lazarus resurrection narrative, and he does not bother to mention the disciples' reaction to the resurrection. We do, however, recognize the disciples' inability to understand the words of Jesus when He spoke about the "glorification of God and the Son of God" (11:4), "twelve hours in the day" (11:9), and "sleep" (11:11). The disciples, while with Jesus during His

---

[363] Elwell and Beitzel, "Mary," *Baker Encyclopedia of the Bible*, 1412.

[364] John MacArthur, *Twelve Extraordinary Women: How God Shaped Women of the Bible, and What He Wants to Do with You* (Nashville: Thomas Nelson Publishers, 2005), 161.

[365] MacArthur, 156.

[366] Michaels and Gasque, 203.

earthly ministry, frequently failed to comprehend His words. I can only surmise that their reaction at Lazarus's resurrection scene was unnecessary to John's writing purpose since the focus seems to be on the Jews' belief and their actions to inform the Pharisees of the miraculous sign performed by Jesus (11:45–57).

John uses the term *Jews* to describe the Jewish people, particularly those in Judea who were hostile to Jesus and his claims (10:39).[367] We can speculate that some of the disciples (unnamed) could have been present during the Feast of Dedication in which the Jews tried to stone Jesus (10:31, 39; 11:8). The Jews in the narrative before verse 47 are different from the chief priests and Pharisees in verse 47. Malina and Rohrbaugh suggest that, throughout the gospel, "faith is one of John's antilanguage terms for loyalty."[368] The ambiguity is obvious because, on the one hand, we are told they believe, and then we are informed that some went and told the Pharisees. Culpepper suggests that John uses the term *Jews* to characterize the people who were indecisive in their actions "as some believe while others plot Jesus' death."[369] Perhaps we will simply refer to the glossary, defining *Jews*, and agree with Smith that the term *Jews* (*Ioudaioi*) is more than simply Judeans or residents of Judea, but inclusive of "people who on religious ground are opposed to Jesus."[370] Let us now consider some of the dialogue between the characters before the resurrection of Lazarus.

---

[367] Kostenberger, *John*, 329.

[368] Malina and Rohrbaugh, 202.

[369] Culpepper, *Anatomy of the Fourth Gospel*, 25.

[370] D. Moody Smith, *The Theology of the Gospel of John* (Cambridge: University Press, 1995), 30.

Dialogue: Prior to Bethany with Disciples, Misunderstanding of Sleep and Resurrection, Martha, and Mary at Bethany

John, the writer, gives us the response of Jesus to the news of Lazarus's being sick in 11:4, which lets the reader have insight into the ultimate purpose of Lazarus's sickness. However, the phrase "this sickness is not unto death" (11:4) must have sounded like good news to those listening and perhaps even soothed the minds of His disciples, who would later react to Jesus's statement, "Let us go to Judea again" (11:7). There appears to be a contradiction in that Jesus stays two more days rather than going immediately to the one He loves (11:6). Moloney contends that it is "actually out of love, Jesus stays for the glory of God to be revealed."[371] The writer does not give us any information regarding what Jesus did during the two days. Still, I suspect he wants us to understand the time difference between Jesus's travel and Lazarus's dead body. This additional time at Bethany beyond the Jordan sets the stage for a greater manifestation and revelation of the glory of God in the resurrection of Lazarus. Kanagaraj supports this contention by writing, "This delay is due to Jesus' commitment to work in God's time so that God's glory may be revealed magnificently in human powerlessness and that his disciple may believe in him (11:15, 40, 42, 45; cf. 11:48)."[372]

Jesus's declaration in 11:7, "Let us go to Judea again," starts a conversation between Jesus and the disciples. The disciples remember the attempted assassination in 10:31 and 39 and question going back to Judea. Jesus gives a brief discourse on day and night that could apply to Himself and the disciples. Carson advocates "that Jesus is safe as long as he performs his Father's will. The daylight period of

---

[371] Moloney, 293.

[372] Jey J. Kanagaraj, *John: A New Covenant Commentary* (Eugene, OR: Cascade Books, 2013), 115.

his ministry may be far advanced, but it is wrong to quit before the twelve hours have been filled up. The time will come soon enough when he will not be able to work."[373] The implication of verse 9 regarding the disciples is that they can perform the assigned work while having Jesus with them before His departure.[374]

The ambiguous statement in 11:11, "Our friend Lazarus sleeps, but I go that I may wake him up," reveals a misunderstanding of the words of Jesus in respect to *sleep* and *dead*. According to Blomberg,

> The verb *koimaomai* denotes literal sleep four times and death fourteen times in its eighteen New Testament occurrences (Morris 1995: 481, n. 24). It was a standard metaphor for death in both the Jewish and Graeo-Roman worlds of Jesus' day (Lindars 1972: 394; Borchert 1996: 352; each with key texts).[375]

Latourelle supports Blomberg's position on the usage of *sleep,* saying, "This is not an unusual use of the term 'fall asleep': of the eighteen times it is used in the New Testament it refers on four occasions to natural sleep and the other fourteen to the sleep of death. In this story then, it has its most frequent New Testament meaning."[376] The term *sleep* about a "dead" person and especially regarding waking a person was not commonly understood in this respect. I believe it was after the resurrection of Jesus that the term *sleep* was associated commonly with "death." Kanagaraj explains that "to fall asleep was used in Judaism and in Christian circles as a euphemism for death (1 Cor. 15:6; 1 Thess. 4:14–16). The narrator clarifies that Jesus means that Lazarus is dead (11:13)."[377]

---

[373] Carson, 409.

[374] Ibid.

[375] Blomberg, 167.

[376] Latourelle, 235.

[377] Kanagaraj, 116.

This statement by Jesus clarifies the misunderstanding of the term *sleep*, but I suspect the disciples are still in the dark as to how Jesus will awaken Lazarus or how this sleep-death will prompt their belief. Thomas gives insight into the disciples' mindset when he states, "Let us also go, that we may die with Him" (11:16). The disciples are thinking of death instead of life, and this statement (11:16) illustrates their failure to grasp that Jesus is life. Let us now move to Bethany and the conversation among Jesus, Martha, and Mary.

The writer again gives us background information before the dialogue with Martha (11:17–20). I agree with Brown concerning 11:17 that "the time indicators are given to show that Lazarus is dead and the deliberate character of Jesus' actions."[378] The details of the location of Bethany being close to Jerusalem help explain why the Jews were there mourning with the family.

After hearing of Jesus's coming, Martha, goes to Him and gives what some in a Western world would call a mild rebuke in 11:21: "Lord if You had been here, my brother would not have died." However, Bultmann contends "that Martha [in] verse 21 gives a painful regret as opposed to a rebuke."[379] Carson also agrees that Martha's words to Jesus are not a rebuke but a mixture of grief and faith, in that she believes Jesus would have healed Lazarus if He had been there.[380] Martha's statement in 11:22 on the surface appears to suggest a resurrection-type faith, but this interpretation is contrary to verse 39.

When Jesus states in 11:23, "Your brother will rise again," it changes the direction of the conversation to a Christological perspective of the current and future realities of life over death. Martha misunderstands the words of Jesus as suggesting the general resurrection (11:24), and perhaps this is also due to what Jesus said in 5:28. Jesus in verses 25–26 redirects Martha's attention from

---

[378] Brown, *The Gospel and Epistles of John*, 61.
[379] Bultmann, 401.
[380] Carson, 412.

the normal Jewish teaching to a current reality of having faith in Him who has the power to grant a life in the future and the current situation. The core of life and resurrected life is dependent on Him alone, so Jesus states emphatically, "I am the resurrection and the life" (11:25). Culpepper believes that "Jesus pulls the hope of the resurrection from the future to the present. Eternal life begins now for those who believe in Jesus Christ."[381]

Martha's response in 11:27, while appearing to be an example of full faith in Jesus as the Christ, fails based on later statements in the narrative (11:39). She fails to understand that Jesus is the resurrection and the life, and He can awaken Lazarus.[382] Michaels and Gasque suggest that Martha's confession in verse 27 is what the writer wants his reader to focus on, which points to the purpose in writing the Gospel.[383] Kanagaraj states, "Martha's testimony in verse 27 has Christological meaning and is the basic belief of God's new community."[384] Her testimony in verse 27 covers the subject of belief in Jesus as the Christ (Anointed One) and the Son of God (revelation of God in the flesh); however, it is debatable whether this faith is manifested in her current situation with the death of Lazarus.

John discusses the action of the Jews and their manner of thinking (11:31) to support further how often characters in his writing misunderstood words and events about Jesus. Mary's response to the news that the "Teacher has come and is calling for you" (11:28) fits perfectly with Luke's material in 10:39, showing her devotion to Jesus by falling at His feet. She quotes almost verbatim the same words as Martha: "Lord, if you had been here, my brother would not have died" (11:32). Blomberg also agrees with me that Mary's reaction to Jesus before the resurrection fits her devotion to Him as outlined

---

[381] Culpepper, *The Gospel and Letters of John*, 183.

[382] Blomberg, 168.

[383] Michaels and Gasque, 203.

[384] Kanagaraj, 117.

in Luke 10:39.[385] Interestingly, John inserts verse 33 regarding the emotional actions of Jesus. In response to Mary and the Jews, Jesus "groaned in the spirit and was troubled" (11:33).

Several theologians have commented on the meaning of Jesus's reaction. Brown states that "Jesus is troubled at this grief; indeed the Greek seems to imply anger (perhaps at her lack of faith, or perhaps in the presence of the suffering caused by the prince of death; see 13:21)."[386] Bultmann advocates that "Jesus is agitated over the lack of faith expressed by the wailing and weeping over Lazarus. They are displaying a lack of faith in Jesus as the Resurrection and Life."[387] Michaels and Gasque believe that Jesus's reaction in verses 33, 35, and 38 all express anger at death and uncleanness. "He was angry at death, the Enemy who holds all human beings' captive to uncleanness and shame (cf. Heb. 2:14–15)."[388]

There are several interpretations of verse 33 concerning the response of Jesus, and I believe it is safe to say that Jesus displayed His humanity while maintaining His deity. Perhaps we would be wise to pattern ourselves after Jesus when we witness the effects of sin, sickness, death, and a visible display of a lack of belief in Jesus Christ. Let us now address the miracle of the resurrection of Lazarus.

Explanation of the Miracle

John informs the reader that the body of Lazarus has been in the grave for four days, which would be long enough for the body to start decaying and stinking (11:39). He has previously informed us that Jesus stayed two more days in Bethany on the other side of the Jordan (11:6), which suggests that even if Jesus had traveled to

---

[385] Blomberg, 169.

[386] Brown, *The Gospel and Epistles of John*, 61.

[387] Bultmann, 406.

[388] Michaels and Gasque, 203.

Bethany near Jerusalem, Lazarus would have still died. Michaels and Gasque tell us that "the purpose of mentioning the four days is to provide a backdrop for Martha's comment in verse 39, and thus for Jesus' dramatic encounter with the grim reality of death in verses 40–44."[389]

The grim reality of death seems to tie in with a "rabbinic belief that the soul hovers over the body of the deceased person for the first three days, intending to re-enter it, but as soon as it sees its appearance change, i.e. that decomposition has set in, it departs (Leviticus Rabbah [a rabbinical commentary]18:1 [on Lv. 15:1])."[390] Kanagaraj also supports this by commenting, "When Jesus arrives there, he finds Lazarus having been in the tomb for four days, a length of time by which, as per Jewish belief, the soul would have left the body, and the body would have fully decayed, making it impossible to recognize the person."[391] Lazarus's length of time in the grave dispels the Jewish belief of the soul reentering the body and magnifies the uniqueness of the miracle that Jesus performed.

We have made a few comments concerning verse 35, "Jesus wept," but I want to take another look at what several theologians suggest this expression means. Kanagaraj's position is that

> Jesus' emotions, mixed with his compassion for the bereaved, made him weep along with them. The Greek word *dokruein*, used in the aorist tense form Jesus' weeping, is different from the word that is used in the present tense for Mary's and the Jews' weeping (*klaiein*). This means that Jesus did not join in the mourners' continual crying, but that he "burst into tears" out of his pity for the bereaved (11:35). He wept with those who wept (Rom. 12:15)![392]

---

[389] Michaels and Gasque, 200.

[390] Carson, 411.

[391] Kanagaraj, 116.

[392] Kanagaraj, 118.

When Jesus wept (11:35), it was an indication of His genuine humanity and physical emotions.[393] Bultmann says that "Jesus wept over the faithlessness of the people present—not over the death of Lazarus."[394] I tend to agree with Bultmann's and Carson's view that Jesus's tears are not shed for Lazarus, based on John 11:11. Jesus's tears are probably due to the impact of sin, death, unbelief, and the people's continuous weeping as if there is no hope. In essence, Jesus is crying on behalf of them and not necessarily in the same manner as they did.[395]

Stones were used to cover the graves' opening so that animals would not invade and ravage the corpus. John inserts the words of Jesus, "Take away the stone" (11:39), perhaps to contrast what would occur at the tomb of Jesus. At Lazarus's grave, humans remove the stone so that a resurrected Lazarus can come out, whereas, at Jesus's tomb, angels remove the stone so that people can come in and view an empty tomb. Martha's objection to Jesus's request to take away the stone (11:39) is an indicator that she did not fully understand what Jesus said about being "the resurrection and the life" (11:25) or the manifestation of the glory of God. The removal of the stone was a step in the process of seeing the glory of God manifested by the resurrection of Lazarus.

Jesus's prayer before the resurrection of Lazarus is an expression of thanksgiving to the Father and an announcement of His being an emissary of God for the belief of the people. Culpepper advocates that "the prayer to the Father is a thank you—signifying to the people of what is about to happen is an act of God."[396] Michaels and Gasque support the relationship connection between Jesus and the Father by stating, "He prays aloud, not because it is necessary, but so that the onlookers will know that he is not acting autonomously. He

---

[393] Blomberg, 169.
[394] Bultmann, 407.
[395] Carson, 416.
[396] Culpepper, *The Gospel and Letters of John*, 183.

calls Lazarus by name, with an authority given him from the Father (cf. 5:21, 25–26)."[397]

The loud command by Jesus, "Lazarus come forth" (11:43), is a simple and specific directive toward Lazarus so that he would rise from the grave and the public could witness this miracle. Latourelle combines the resurrection of Lazarus with the "loose him and let him go" (11:44) command, stating that

> the manner of Jesus's intervention is consistent with his habitual manner of acting: his action is reduced to a simple command ("Lazarus, come out") and to a sign ("Unbind him"), which is meant to show that the return to life is fully real (similarly, he asked that Jairus' daughter be given something to eat: Lk. 8:55).[398]

Kostenberger states that the loud shout of Jesus was "one of raw authority (Burge 2000: 320), and the power of his voice expresses the power of God by which the dead are brought back to life (Ridderbos 1997:406)."[399] There was nothing quiet about this command; there was no muttering. It was loud so that all could hear the power of Jesus. I have heard preachers declare the power of Jesus, and I concur that the authority and power of Jesus's spoken words were so great that if He had not specifically called only Lazarus, then all tombs would have given up the dead.[400] This resurrection of Lazarus is a foreshadowing demonstration of the power of Jesus as "the resurrection and the life" (11:25).

The command to "loose him, and let him go" gives further credence to the fact that a man who had been dead for four days was alive for all to see and could return to his daily activities. There is

---

[397] Michaels and Gasque, 204.
[398] Latourelle, 236.
[399] Kostenberger, 345.
[400] Carson, 418.

irony in the words of Jesus because this miraculous sign, according to John's gospel, would ultimately lead to the arrest, trial, and crucifixion of Jesus. In essence, Jesus gives life to a dead man, leading to His giving His own life so that we might believe and live.[401] Lazarus comes out of the tomb with grave-clothes on, which in some ways ties him to this earthly life and future death. We cannot help but remember that when Jesus rose from the grave, there was no need to untie Him to go free because the grave clothes remained in the tomb (20:5–7), and there was no earthly power restraining Him.

Other Miracles Similar to Jesus's Resurrecting Lazarus

Several resurrection narratives appear in the scripture; however, I want to argue against the idea that Luke's Lazarus story (16:19–31) influenced John's writing in chapter 11. The difference is seen in that there is no resurrection of the rich man or Lazarus in Luke's story, so in essence, there should be nothing to compare. Latourelle argues, "In the parable, God refuses to bring the rich man back to earthly life in order that he may warn his brothers, whereas in John the dead man is restored to life."[402] There are other major differences, such as, in Luke's story, the dead man is to return to warn others, but in John's story, Lazarus does not speak. The Lazarus of John's story is not poor, whereas the one in Luke's story is.[403] I do not believe these Lazarus stories are in any way similar.

Kostenberg notes that the

raising of the dead [is] very rare in both the OT and the Gospels. In all four Gospels combined, there are only three such events: the raising of Jairus's daughter (Mark 5:22–24,

---

[401] Brown, *The Gospel and Epistles of John,* 61.
[402] Latourelle, 231.
[403] Ibid.

38–42 pars.); the raising of the widow's son at Nain (Luke 7:11–15); and the raising of Lazarus (John 11:1–44) (M. Harris 1986).[404]

In Mark's story (5:22–24, 38–42) of the "raising of Jairus' daughter; the news of sickness preceded the news of death; just like in John's story. Mary throws herself at His feet as Jairus does in Mk 5:22."[405] In both stories, Jesus uses the term sleep; however, the major difference is the time element: Jairus's daughter was dead less than one day versus the four days of Lazarus being dead and in the grave.

In Luke's story of raising the widow's son at Nain, there are differences from the other resurrection stories, such as Jesus's actions are not requested; He saw and had compassion on her (7:13). Also, He touches the bier (7:14), whereas he asks others to remove the stone (11:39). In Luke's story, Jesus does not appear to be agitated or troubled in spirit due to the people's response to the death of the widow's son. However, in John's writing, He is deeply troubled after conversing with friends He loves and then revealing Himself as "the resurrection and the life" (11:25), and yet they weep as if there is no hope (11:33). Perhaps again, the major difference hinges on the length of time Lazarus is dead and the decay of the physical body.[406]

The Old Testament also contains occurrences of resurrecting bodies: Elijah in 1 Kings 17:17–24 and Elisha in 2 Kings 4:19–36. In both situations, the man of God prays to God to restore life and then lays on the child. These men of God petition God on behalf of the dead person, whereas Jesus speaks with the power of God, giving life to that which was dead. Blomberg again argues that Elijah and Elisha are empowered to revivify recently deceased persons.[407] Elijah and Elisha act as ambassadors for God, whereas in John's gospel,

---

[404] Kostenberger, *John*, 321–322.
[405] Blomberg, 232.
[406] Blomberg, 165.
[407] Ibid.

Jesus is the revelation of God (John 1:1, 14) and life itself. There is the story in 2 Kings 13:20–21 whereby, after Elisha had died and buried, the Moabites were burying a dead man and cast his body upon the body of Elisha, and the dead man stood on his feet. The writer does not give us any more information regarding the man revived. We hesitate to comment further or include this account as a resurrection based upon the limited information available.

The New Testament book of Acts contains two occurrences of resurrections: Peter in Acts 9:36-42 and Paul in Acts 20:9-12. In both situations, the representative of God acts as an intercessor between death and life. Peter knelt and prayed over Dorcas, and Paul embraced the young man, similar to what Elijah and Elisha did in the Old Testament resurrection occurrences. We should also note that these resurrections occurred within a short time of the death, as opposed to Lazarus being dead and buried four days. Jesus spoke with the power of life into the decaying dead corpus of Lazarus. Let us now consider the impact of the resurrection of Lazarus on the immediate audience.

Impact of the Miracle on the Attending Audience

John leaves many questions unanswered concerning the attending audience's reaction to the resurrection of Lazarus, especially in respect to Mary, Martha, Lazarus, and the disciples. Kostenberger questions the silence of Lazarus in contrast to the loud voice of Jesus, and in fact, we are told nothing about a reaction from Lazarus.[408] The writer is silent in terms of the family's response to seeing Lazarus until chapter 12, where he informs us of a dinner party and the anointing of Jesus by Mary. He concludes chapter 11 by focusing on the Jews who believe in Jesus and inform the Pharisees. Several theologians

---

[408] Kostenberger, *John*, 347.

have commented that some of the Jews from Jerusalem believed in Jesus while others went and informed the Pharisees (11:45–46).

Culpepper suggests mixed emotions in the crowd, as some believed while others went and told what had happened, which is similar to the narratives of the man at the pool of Bethesda and the blind man.[409] One could hope that the motive of some of these Jews was to merely inform the Pharisees of the truth of the resurrection of Lazarus. However, considering 11:46–53, the intent of the informers appears to be to incite malicious and deadly activity by the chief priest and Pharisees toward Jesus.[410] Moloney comments that John is "silent regarding the Jews telling the leaders of Jesus statements, resurrection and the life or the prayer that His actions would reveal the glory of God in His being the Sent One."[411] I do not see sufficient reason to believe that the informing Jews did not tell them of Jesus's saying, "I am the resurrection and the life," and how Jesus prayed. However, I would agree with Moloney that the Jewish leaders are more concerned about their position, power, and status than the miraculous sign based upon 11:47–48.[412]

Kanagaraj contends that the Pharisees were "troubled by the religious and political consequences of the mass following of Jesus."[413] John does not tell us how many people believed in Jesus, but it was sufficient to cause an uproar among the Pharisees. What is astonishing is the absolute refusal to believe that Jesus was the sent One from the Father. MacArthur says that the Pharisees' position concerning Jesus is that "they obstinately refused to consider that His power to give life was proof that He was exactly who He claimed to be: God the Son."[414] Perhaps Latourelle summarizes it best: "Miracles

---

[409] Culpepper, *The Gospel and Letters of John*, 183.

[410] Carson, 419.

[411] Moloney, 293.

[412] Ibid.

[413] Kanagaraj, 121.

[414] MacArthur, 158.

are signs given by Christ to guide human beings to the kingdom and urge them to conversion. It takes a setting of grace to accept and acknowledge miracles as signs."[415] While John informs us that the Pharisees identified the miracle as a sign (11:47), there was no "setting of grace" to accept Him as the sent One. According to Culpepper, the Pharisees' response (11:48) is ironic in that Jesus dies, and the Romans still destroy the temple in 70 AD. The high priest is speaking prophesy in 11:49–52 without knowing it.

John concludes this resurrection narrative by informing the reader that Jesus also responds, in 11:54, in that He "no longer walked openly among the Jews but went from there into the country near the wilderness, to a city called Ephraim, and there remained with His disciples." Let us now consider the impact of the resurrection of Lazarus on the church.

Impact of the Miracle on the Church

The Jewish religious leaders were not in attendance during the resurrection of Lazarus; however, their actions and behavior afterward helped shape events leading to the crucifixion of Jesus and the persecution of the early church. John tells us in 12:1–8 that, six days later, a supper is prepared for Jesus and His disciples that Martha serves, Lazarus was in attendance, and Mary anointed Jesus with "very costly oil of spikenard." We get a glimpse of their appreciation for what Jesus had done in resurrecting Lazarus, but we also notice the indifference of Judas Iscariot (12:4–5) toward Mary's act of thanksgiving. What is interesting is the fact that Lazarus is silent during all these events; we never hear anything from him.

Lockyer suggests that perhaps the reason we do not hear from him later in New Testament scripture is that he "was forced to flee, seeing that the infuriated elders determined his death (John 12:10–

---

[415] Latourelle, 316.

11). With a deep affection for his Friend, Lazarus would withdraw more for His sake than for his own. He felt his presence only increased the Master's danger."[416] Lincoln believes that

> Lazarus has not only attracted, on the negative side, a parallel death plot, he has also, on the positive side, become almost a rival object of attention to Jesus! The resurrected Lazarus is the primary public exhibit of Jesus' extraordinary powers. The language employed for the effect produced by Lazarus may reflect the later situation of the rivalry between the synagogue and the Johannine community—on his account, many of the Jews were going away and believing in Jesus.[417]

The gospel of John does not support Lockyer's opinion; however, I would conclude that additional information and even oral communication from Lazarus was not the focus and purpose of his writing as outlined in 20:31. It is reasonable to believe that the impact of the resurrected Lazarus could have prompted many Jews to abandon the synagogue in favor of faith in Jesus.

Questions have been raised regarding the authenticity of the narrative of the resurrection of Lazarus, specifically by John Shelby Spong, in that Lazarus is not mentioned by name in any of the Johannine Christian sources. His opinion is that "in the Lazarus story, told in John 11, every symbol employed by John reveals that Lazarus is not a person, but a sign and a symbol."[418] I struggle with the Spong theory because it does not make sense for John to include a symbolic narrative of the resurrection of Lazarus that, in essence, led to the crucifixion of Jesus. This type of thinking leads to questioning

---

[416] Herbert Lockyer, *All the Men of the Bible* (Grand Rapids, MI: Zondervan Publishing House, 1958), 216.

[417] Lincoln, 341.

[418] John Shelby Spong, *The Fourth Gospel: Tales of a Jewish Mystic* (New York: HarperCollins Publishers, 2013), 153.

and even doubting all the miracles within John's writing, which undermines the validity of the gospel and the identity of our Lord Jesus Christ.

Barrett contends, "There is no parallel in any other gospel to the Johannine narrative as it stands (there are resurrection stories in Mark 5:21–43; Matt. 9:18–26; Luke 8:40–56; Luke 7:11–16); this, however, need not in itself mean that the narrative was created by John."[419] Latourelle agrees with Barrett, writing,

> John's starting point is not a fiction but a real action of Jesus. This action is charged with an intelligibility so great that it eludes conceptualization. Jesus caused a human being to pass from death to life: this qualitative leap produced within our world is the basis for presenting Jesus as the Absolute Being who is the source of life and Life. The truth is seen in his attention to details of places, persons, distance, and contemporary custom.[420]

Keener notes that "Meier provides convincing evidence that the Lazarus story goes back to John's tradition, though it was originally a brief story unrelated to Jesus' passion. Hence, he does not regard it as surprising that the Synoptics omit it."[421] Furthermore, third-century rabbis concede these people rising from the dead but credit them to necromancy.[422] One thing evident in John's writing is that this resurrection story is a critical element in developing the plot by the chief priest and Pharisees to kill Jesus. According to Bultmann, the resurrection of Lazarus is "the greatest of the miracle accounts and is at the beginning of the passion of Jesus."[423] I will opt to agree

---

[419] Barrett, 389.
[420] Latourelle, 232.
[421] Keener, 836.
[422] Ibid.
[423] Bultmann, 395.

with Barrett, Blomberg, Latourelle, and Keener that the resurrection of Lazarus is an authentic story, not to mention the longest of the miraculous sign narratives within John's gospel.

The resurrection of Lazarus has helped to shape Christian viewpoints on the power of Jesus Christ to impart life to those who are dead spiritually and physically. According to Culpepper, this seventh sign portrays Jesus as the giver of life to those who believe in Him.[424] It is visible evidence of His being the "the resurrection and the life" (11:25), and this is critical for those who would later suffer persecution and death for their faith in Jesus Christ. Michaels says that this narrative of Jesus's resurrecting Lazarus puts "Himself, and faith in him, squarely at the center of the resurrection hope, and he transforms that hope from a future, somewhat theoretical, expectation into a present experience of the very life of God."[425] Barrett argues the position that "the raising of Lazarus is no piece of black magic or even the supreme achievement of a saint; it is an anticipation of what is to take place at the last day. It means that the believer has eternal life; that he has passed from death into life."[426] This is the position of the believer in Jesus Christ, as Kanagaraj explains: "This means that in Jesus the eternally existing God reveals himself as the one who offers to those who believe in Jesus the life of resurrection now and at the end-time."[427] The length of time in which a believer has been dead in Jesus Christ makes no difference; just as with Lazarus, so shall it be with the dead in Christ. Paul declares our final victory in 1 Corinthians 15:57: "But thanks be to God, who gives us the victory through our Lord Jesus Christ." Let us now consider whether the narrative of the resurrection of Lazarus provides sufficient proof of the deity of Jesus Christ.

---

[424] Culpepper, *The Gospel and Letters of John*, 183.

[425] Michaels and Gasque, 202.

[426] Barrett, 388.

[427] Kanagaraj, 117.

Whether This Sign Gives Sufficient Reason to Believe Jesus Is the Son of God

I believe this miraculous sign of the resurrection of Lazarus furnishes ample reasons to believe that Jesus is the Son of God, and I have outlined several thoughts for consideration.

1) The resurrection of Lazarus has a uniqueness to which other resuscitations or resurrections are not equivalent. Keener noted that in the ancient Mediterranean culture, sorcerers might have resuscitated corpses. Still, they did so at night, and many reports included drilling holes and pouring hot blood into the bodies.[428] This type of attempt to resurrect a body is unequal to what Jesus did at the grave of Lazarus, where He said, "Lazarus come forth" (11:43). The uniqueness of the resurrection of Lazarus is further unmatched in terms of the length of time the person was dead. In the Old Testament accounts of Elijah and Elisha, respectively (1 Kings 17:17–24 and 2 Kings 4:19–36), both individuals had died recently and cannot be compared to being dead for four days (John 11:39). The length of time that Lazarus was dead stands in sharp contrast to even the resurrection by Jesus of Jairus's daughter (Mark 5:22–29, 38–42), the raising of the widow's son in Nain (Luke 7:11–15), the resurrection of Dorcas by Peter in Joppa (Acts 9:36-43), and the raising of Eutychus by Paul (Acts 20:9-12). The notable difference between Lazarus's resurrection and other New Testament resurrections is the length of time Lazarus was dead and his body decayed.

2) The present witnesses and the curious witnesses indirectly acknowledge the power of Jesus to give life to a dead man.

---

[428] Keener, *A Commentary*, 837.

John 11:45 states, "Then many of the Jews who had come to Mary, and had seen the things Jesus did, believed in Him." Latourelle advocates that

> recognition of the miracles of Jesus is inseparable to the identification of Christ as Son of the Father, it presupposes that grace exerts its action not only in the confession of faith but all along the journey that leads through signs to the recognition of Jesus of Nazareth as Messiah and Son of the Father.[429]

John inserts in 12:8–12 the plot to kill Lazarus due to the resurrection, and again he tells us, "Many of the Jews went away and believed in Jesus." The implication is that many Jews in Bethany and perhaps some from Jerusalem began to believe in Jesus. If we read the words in 11:45 at face value, we must accept that they accomplished what John desired in his purpose in writing, as noted in 20:31.

3) The words of Jesus and the execution of the resurrection of Lazarus are the justification of His deity. Jesus demonstrates His commitment to the will of God in delaying the trip to Bethany and then declaring, "This sickness is not unto death, but for the glory of God that the Son of God may be glorified through it" (11:4). He further reveals Himself as the "resurrection and the life" and prompts Martha and Mary to believe in Him as the life-giver. Michaels and Gasque assert that "the distinctly Christian note here is that Jesus will raise them. He, in his own person, is the resurrection and, therefore, the life. Eternal life is a relationship to him."[430] Perhaps this is the essence of what

---

[429] Latourelle, 318.

[430] Michaels and Gasque, 202.

Jesus said in 11:26—that whoever lives and believes in Him has eternal life. The "I am" words of Jesus remind us of 1:4, but then these words set the stage for the command, "Lazarus, come forth," which highlights the power of His words. Brown states that this is the "fulfillment of Jesus's prophecy from John 5:28 — 'for the hour is coming in which all who are in the tombs shall hear his voice."[431] The resurrections of the Old Testament and those in the early church include the ambassadors of God praying to God for restoration of the person. Jesus merely gives thanks to God for hearing Him and indicates that the prayer was simply for the audience's benefit. The words and actions of Jesus become the justification for satisfying our belief that He is the Christ and Son of God.

---

[431] Brown, *The Gospel and Epistles of John*, 61.

CHAPTER 10

Debatable Signs

Jesus Cleanses the Temple

The gospel of John (2:13–22) and the Synoptic Gospels (Matt. 21:12–17, Mark 11:15–19, Luke 19:45–48) contain the debatable sign of Jesus cleansing the temple. Whereas John inserts this narrative at the beginning of Jesus's ministry, after the miracle of turning water to wine, the Synoptic Gospels show it was occurring at the end of Jesus's ministry and leading to His arrest and death by crucifixion. It is not within this project's scope to address the various opinions on whether Jesus cleanses the temple more than once or the chronological correctness of John versus the Synoptics. Carson tells us, "Most scholars argue that John has moved the account to the beginning of Jesus's ministry perhaps because he sees in this cleansing a prophetic and programmatic action that explicates so much of what he will develop."[432] We will limit our discussion to the actual event of cleansing the temple, the reaction

---

[432] Carson, 177.

of the immediate audience to this event, and whether it satisfies the definition of a miraculous sign.

John informs us that the season is the Passover of the Jews, during which Jesus is going to Jerusalem. Kostenberger reminds us that Jewish men were taught to celebrate Passover in Jerusalem (Deut. 16:16).[433] Carson suggests that the Passover of the Jews received this label because the residents of Judea were called Jews by the Galileans and the Diaspora Hebrews.[434] Jesus, being a Jew, would naturally attend this most important annual feast in Jerusalem, the capital city located at a higher elevation than Galilee.[435] For the Jews particularly, Jerusalem was considered the center of the world, and people would have to travel uphill because Jerusalem was in the mountains (cf. Ps 125:2; Acts 11:2; 15:1; 18:22).[436]

The scene in which Jesus cleanses the temple notably involves the temple's outer court,[437] which, in essence, "had come to resemble a market rather than a place of worship. The scene can be contrasted directly with the Old Testament prophetic view of the role of the temple in the worship of God (e.g., Zech. 14:20–21; Mic 6:6–13; Jer. 7:4)."[438] Carson writes, "Instead of solemn dignity and the murmur of prayer, there is the bellowing of cattle and the bleating of sheep. Instead of brokenness and contrition, holy adoration and prolonged petition, there is noisy commerce."[439] In the Synoptic passages of Matthew 21:13, Mark 11:17, and Luke 19:46, Jesus describes the temple activity as making it "a den of thieves" as opposed to a house of prayer. Kostenberger perhaps best summarizes the temple scene:

---

[433] Kostenberger, *John*, 104.
[434] Carson, 176.
[435] Ibid.
[436] Borchert, 162.
[437] Kostenberger, *John*, 105.
[438] Ibid., 163.
[439] Carson, 176.

In Jesus' day the temple had become a Jewish "nationalistic stronghold," a place where Gentile worship was obstructed. This ran counter to the original Solomonic vision (cf. Kings 8:41–43). By selling sacrificial animals and setting up their currency exchange in the court of the Gentiles, the outer court of the temple, the merchants in effect torpedoed Gentile worship in the only place where it was possible.[440]

We could make the case that Jesus cleanses the temple because of the exclusion of Gentile worship and focuses on the selling of animals plus the exchange of currency.

John 2:15 informs us that Jesus made a "whip of cords" and drove out the sheep and oxen. Vincent calls the whip "a rope of twisted rushes."[441] Jamieson suggests that the small cords were "likely some of the rushes spread for bedding, and when twisted used to tie up the cattle there collected."[442] John does not tell us where or how Jesus acquired the whip of cords, only that He made one and drove them all out. The implication in reading 2:15 is that Jesus could have used the whip of cords on the animals and perhaps even the people; however, John does not specifically say how Jesus used it.

Simeon comments that to correct the evil of the temple, "our Lord exerted his divine authority. He drove out the cattle and ordered the doves to be removed. He overturned the tables of money and commanded all the traders to depart; nor did any of the people dare to oppose his sovereign command."[443] Simeon states that this event

---

[440] Kostenberger, *John*, 103.

[441] M. R. Vincent, *Word Studies in the New Testament*, Vol. 2 (New York: Charles Scribner's Sons, 1887), 84.

[442] R. Jamieson, A. R. Fausset, and D. Brown. *Commentary Critical and Explanatory on the Whole Bible*, Vol. 2 (Oak Harbor, WA: Logos Research Systems, Inc., 1997), 130.

[443] C. Simeon, *Horae Homileticae: Luke XVII to John XII*, Vol. 13 (London: Holdsworth and Ball, 1833), 237–238.

in the temple was a demonstration of the divine power of Jesus over the minds of the people present.[444]

> He did this singly, unarmed, unsupported, and in opposition to the existing authorities: yet behold, they were all constrained to yield submission to his will. We cannot doubt but that he miraculously overawed their minds: nor was this a less exertion of omnipotence than any other of the miracles which he wrought.[445]

Jamieson and Simeon suggest that the departure from the temple resulted from the miraculous power of Jesus's spoken word. Jamieson also supports Simeon by stating that "not by this slender whip but by divine majesty was the ejection accomplished, the whip being but a sign of the scourge of divine anger." Spence advocates that "the 'scourge,' as Godet says, is a symbol, not an instrument. It was in Christ's hands a conspicuous method of expressing his indignation, and augmenting the force of his command by an indication that he meant to be obeyed there and then."[446] I would agree that this concept is possible; however, it would mean that John, as the writer, missed an opportunity to identify and highlight the deity of Jesus Christ through the spoken word to cleanse the temple. Furthermore, it becomes argumentative to claim that Jesus drove the animals and people from the temple with the spoken word but physically poured out the money and turned the tables over (2:15). When we consider the actual text, I believe John is silent concerning the details of Jesus's actions with the whip of cords as this is not essential to his overall narrative purpose.

The declaration by Jesus in 2:16 expresses a direct command and a law concerning His Father's house. Kendall advocates that the

---

[444] Ibid.

[445] Simeon, 237–237.

[446] H. D. M. Spence-Jones, ed., *Gospel of John*, Vol. 17, (Peabody, MA: 1909), 89.

design of the temple and the sacred items in it were erected with a focus on prayer—from the altar for sacrifice to the basin, table, lampstand, and even incense.[447] In the Synoptic Gospels' accounts of Jesus cleansing the temple (Matt.21:13, Mark 11:17, Luke 19:46), He identifies the house by saying, "My house is a house of prayer." Perhaps this misuse of the temple is what prompted Jesus to give this command in John 2:16.

Gebbert comments, "We cannot be sure what upsets Jesus most. Perhaps it is an exclusive Jewish nationalism that has no place for Gentile worship. Perhaps it is profiteering by the officials. Perhaps it is simply the commercialism of it all, crowding out worship."[448] Carson states that there was no evidence of corruption on the part of the merchants and money-changers, but rather the main focus was that these activities should not be in the temple, period.[449] We can see that "there was nothing wrong in the merchandise; but to bring it, for their own and others' convenience, into that most sacred place, was a high-handed profanation which the eye of Jesus could not endure."[450] John's gospel narrative does not focus on whether the business activity was corrupt, whereas, in the Synoptics, Jesus calls it a den of thieves. John's focus seems aimed at the concept of turning the Lord's house into a place of merchandise as opposed to a place of worship and prayer. Kostenberger states, "Jesus faulted the merchants for disrupting Gentile worship in the only place that was open to them—the so-called court of the Gentiles—which was insensitive at best and evidence of religious arrogance at worst."[451]

John informs the reader that "the disciples recognized that Jesus was intolerant (zealous) when it came to the misuse of God's place

---

[447] R. T. Kendall, *Understanding Theology*, Vol. 2 (Ross-shire, Great Britain: Christian Focus, 2000), 173–174.

[448] T. J. Geddert, *Mark* (Scottdale, PA: Herald Press, 2001), 265.

[449] Carson, 178–179.

[450] Jamieson, Fausset, and Brown, 130.

[451] Kostenberger, *John*, 106.

by the religious leaders (John 2:17)."[452] "In this text, the disciples are said to have viewed the action as righteous indignation and indeed as the fulfillment of Scripture (2:17; cf. Ps 69:9)."[453] Michaels questions whether the disciples remember the scripture citation at the time of the cleansing as most commentators suppose or whether they remembered it later after the resurrection.[454] The gospel of John shows many misunderstandings of Jesus's words by the disciples and the Jews, so they probably remembered the citation later. However, we must recognize that John notes the disciples' reaction first and before the Jews in verse 18. It is not inconceivable that the disciples remembered Psalm 69:9 at the time of Jesus's pronouncement. I must also note that just because the disciples might have remembered the scripture or even accepted His actions, this does not connect the dots in terms of recognizing the deity of Jesus.

The Jews' reaction differs from the disciples' reaction in that they request a sign from Jesus as evidence of His right to cleanse the temple (2:18). The religious authorities ignore Jesus's reference to "my Father's house" (v. 16) and focus on the action performed.[455] Carson claims that the temple representatives of the council knew this was no ordinary person and wanted evidence of His authority to take such action in the temple.[456] Kostenberger suggests that it is not uncommon for people to want proof of a prophet's legitimacy.[457] Borchert mentions that these Jews (2:18) were probably keepers of order in the temple and merely challenging Jesus to justify His actions.[458]

---

[452] Borchert, 163–164.

[453] Ibid.

[454] Michaels, 162.

[455] Michaels, 163.

[456] Carson, 181.

[457] Kostenberger, *John*, 108.

[458] Borchert, 165.

The irony of their request is that Jesus must have performed other signs not recorded by John, particularly when reading of His conversation with Nicodemus 3:2. If Nicodemus was aware of Jesus's signs based upon God being with Him, surely the keepers of order in the temple were also aware. The Jews in the temple had missed the sign, which is indicative of their spiritual blindness. If the authorities had remembered the Old Testament Scriptures, they would have recognized the cleansing of the temple as a sign of the coming Messiah.[459]

The dialogue between Jesus and the Jews in verses 19–22 renders another example of the misunderstanding of Jesus's words. We know that Jesus is referring to His death and resurrection after three days (2:19). However, the Jews literally interpret the words of Jesus even though they are symbolic and filled with theological meaning.[460] Jesus's response to their request for a sign is a challenge for the Jews to destroy the temple, and in three days, He will raise it up. Jesus is challenging them to kill Him, and in three days, He will rise again. But because the Jews misunderstand Jesus, they focus on the literal temple and the length of time required to build it. John inserts narrator comments in verses 21–22 so that future readers know the meaning of verse 19. We will now turn our attention to the question of whether the cleansing of the temple satisfies the definition of a miraculous sign that encourages faith in Jesus as the Son of God.

The cleansing of the temple by Jesus satisfies the definition of a sign as documented in the glossary. Recall that the *Baker Encyclopedia of the Bible* describes signs as "connoting a visible event intended to convey meaning beyond that which is normally perceived in the outward appearance of the event."[461] The clarification of the event is given in the explanation by Jesus in verses 16 and 19. It is from Jesus's explanations that we can surmise that the temple belongs to

---

[459] Carson, 181.

[460] Kostenberger, *John*, 109.

[461] Elwell and Beitzel, *Baker Encyclopedia of the Bible*, Vol. 2, 1961.

His Father and should be a place for prayer and communion with God. We are also aware of the double meaning of the word *temple* in reference to Jesus's body. Jesus is prophesying His death and resurrection, which will be the ultimate and only sign given.

I must argue that this cleansing of the temple does not satisfy the definition of a miracle according to Myers, who describes a miracle as "an event remarkable in that it goes contrary to the laws of nature, that is, to the usual course of events."[462] Lange contends that "John relates the purging of the temple alone as the first characteristic work, the signal-miracle of the Lord on His public appearance."[463] Simeon suggests that Jesus used miraculous power over the minds of men in the temple.[464] But the writer, John, does not suggest or scripturally support this position. I cannot recall any event in Scripture whereby Jesus used divine power to manipulate the minds of men. I would even argue that this theory runs counter to the ideology of free choice that God gives to humankind.

I would conclude that John inserted this event as a sign to those open to seeing the Christology of Jesus's cleansing the temple. Our Lord Jesus requires sanctification, which would have been essential during the temple worship at Passover season.

The Large Catch of Fish

The gospel of John (21:1–14) records a narrative of Jesus commanding His disciples to "cast the net on the right side of the boat" to catch fish. Another fish-catching narrative appears in Luke 5:1–11 and can be compared to John's writing. In both John's and Luke's narratives, the disciples witness a revelation of Jesus. I will argue that the revelation is more deliberate in John's narrative, which

---

[462] Myers, 722.

[463] Lange and Schaff, 115.

[464] Simeon, 238.

correlates to the purpose of persuading the reader to have faith in Jesus Christ, the Son of God. The narrative begins in 21:1, telling us that "Jesus showed Himself again to the disciples," which suggests that all the activity after that revealed Jesus as the person crucified but resurrected according to His prophetic words (2:19).

Our objective will be to discuss various details of the narrative related to the sign and then address whether this fish-catching event qualifies as a miraculous sign in the gospel of John. It is not within our purpose to address the authorship of this chapter or its inclusion within the gospel. Let us begin with the scene for this narrative.

The writer identifies the location as being "at the Sea of Tiberias." (21:1) "the Roman designation for the Sea of Galilee (cf. 6:1), a place also called the Sea of Genessaret as in Luke 5:1 and the Sea of Chinnereth (Num 34:11), from the Hebrew *kinnerot/kinneret* meaning "harp."[465] The Sea of Tiberias is the same sea written about in 6:1, and I would argue that the disciples were familiar with fishing in this body of water. Carver informs us that the Sea of Tiberias was a major economic resource for fishing and the central location for many of Jesus's teachings.[466] It is at this familiar land and body of water that Jesus chooses to reveal Himself again to His disciples after His crucifixion and resurrection from the grave. The gospel writer had previously recorded in 20:19 and 26 instances whereby Jesus came to His disciples behind locked doors and revealed Himself; now, this revelation is outdoors along the Sea of Tiberias.

The gospel writer informs us of seven and possibly eight disciples (if you include the author separate from the two unnamed disciples) present for this showing of Jesus. Michaels comments that Simon Peter is mentioned first because he will be the first to speak (v. 3).[467] Carson suggests that Simon Peter is the unofficial leader of

---

[465] Borchert, 323.
[466] Carver, "Galilee, Sea of, Archaeology of," *The Lexham Bible Dictionary.*
[467] Michaels, 1029.

the disciples since he speaks first in verse 3.[468] Two other disciples are mentioned by name: Thomas, who publicly doubted the resurrection of Jesus (20:25), and Nathanael, whom we learn is from Cana of Galilee, where Jesus performed His first miraculous sign of turning water into wine (2:1–11). Based upon the disciple listing in verse 2, we do not gain any insight into the authorship of this gospel.

The story begins with Peter announcing that he is going fishing, and the disciples who are present join him in fishing at night. We can speculate on why they went fishing (possibility of needing food to eat), but the fact is clear that they were fishing at night and caught nothing. Kostenberger comments that night was the preferred time for fishing because it enabled the fishermen to sell fresh fish the next morning.[469] Keener notes that night fishing is more profitable on the Lake of Galilee than day fishing.[470] Borchert writes that "Brown notes at this point that in the Gospels the disciples never catch fish without Jesus' assistance. Although this phenomenon may be correct, it should not be taken to mean that they were poor fishermen."[471] I would argue that the writer inserts these details to remind us of Jesus's words to His disciples, "for without Me you can do nothing" (15:5).

We cannot help but notice the contrast of night versus morning in verses 3–4, which aligns with the motif of light versus darkness in the prologue of John chapter 1. The inability of the disciples to recognize Jesus could be attributed to the early morning hour or the distance from the shore.[472] Michaels comments that the stage is set for Jesus to reveal Himself, similar to what occurred in 20:19–20 with the disciples and in 20:14 with Mary Magdalene.[473] Jesus initiates the

---

[468] Carson, 668.

[469] Kostenberger, *John*, 589.

[470] Keener, 1227.

[471] Borchert, 326.

[472] Kostenberger, *John*, 589–590.

[473] Michaels, 1031.

conversation in 21:5: "Children, have you any food?" Keener suggests that this question anticipates a negative response and forces them to recognize their insufficient resources based on their abilities.[474]

We are challenged with why the disciples, being experienced fishermen, would obey someone they do not yet recognize on shore. Perhaps Keener is correct in suggesting that there is a moral lesson in obedience before the fuller revelation of Jesus.[475] I would submit that it is possible for them to subconsciously recognize the voice of Jesus from past fishing experiences (Luke 5:4) as well as what Jesus said in 10:4, 14, and 27. In either case, their efforts are rewarded with a large catch of fish (John 21:6). It is at this point that the revelation of whom the stranger is, becomes apparent to the disciple whom Jesus loved, and he says, "It is the Lord!" (21:7). His quick insight in identifying Jesus prompts Simon Peter's quick action to put on his outer garment and go to Jesus.

Newman advocates that "the Greek adjective *gumnos* usually means 'naked,' but it can also mean 'lightly clothed.' This second meaning is indicated here since a Jew would never disrobe completely while fishing."[476] I accept Newman's comments and agree that Peter was not fishing naked but wearing some type of undergarments. John 21:7 states that Peter "put on his outer garment (for he had removed it) and plunged into the sea." The distance to shore was "about two hundred cubits" (21:8), which is "a little over a hundred yards."[477] In essence, Peter's reaction to the announcement, "It is the Lord!" (21:7), prompts him to swim to Jesus instead of waiting and coming with the other disciples in the boat dragging the fish.

John continues the narrative revealing Jesus on the shore of the Sea of Tiberias by identifying the fire of coals and the bread (21:9). The image of the fire of coals in the morning is contrary

---

[474] Keener, 1228.

[475] Ibid.

[476] Newman and Nida, 628.

[477] Vincent, 297.

to the fire of coals in John 18:18 when Peter warmed himself on a cold night while denying being a disciple of Jesus. The attention to detail seems to be deliberate to set the stage for the conversation between Jesus and Peter. Michaels insists that the fire of coals is not for warmth as during the time Peter denied Jesus but rather for cooking fish.[478] Jesus, as the host, had prepared the fire of coals, the fish, and the bread. Keener cautions us against drawing a Eucharistic meaning from this setting by commenting that "the presence of the fish provides no clear Eucharistic overtones, and this passage lacks mention of breaking of bread, drinking, or giving of thanks."[479] Jesus uses no Eucharistic language in John 21:10 and 12. If the intent was to show this as a messianic meal, the author does not declare it in this narrative.

Jesus's instructions to the disciples to "bring some of the fish which you have just caught" (21:10) set the stage for Peter to demonstrate his devotion to the Lord (21:11), as he had previously done by swimming to shore (21:7). Kostenberger comments that Jesus both enables the disciples to catch a large quantity of fish and instructs them to use what they caught.[480] Michaels suggests that perhaps this bringing some of the fish is symbolic of bringing an offering unto the Lord, which most Jews would have been taught from the Old Testament.[481] John implies that Peter alone dragged the net of fish to shore and then counted them, totaling 153. While this exclusive action by Peter is debatable, it would express his renewed devotion after the previous denial and demonstration of a lack of faith.

There are many theories regarding the 153 fish and the fact that the nets did not break. Michaels advocates that "the number is remarkable both because it is very large (in keeping with similar extravagances in 2:6, 6:13, 12:3, and 19:39), and because it is so

---

[478] Michaels, 1035.
[479] Keener, 1231.
[480] Kostenberger, *John*, 592.
[481] Michaels, 1036.

specific without being a round number (like one hundred) or an obviously symbolic one (like twelve)."[482] Blomberg comments,

> Despite numerous attempts to find allegorical significance in the number (all of them relatively far-fetched; see the succinct survey in Carson 1991: 672–673), the best explanation is that the disciples counted them (van der Loos 1965: 677). Likewise, the untorn net (v. 11b) probably does not symbolize the unity of the church. Any symbolism to the church is perhaps they can bring in a large number of disciples.[483]

Kanagaraj notes that a large number of fish symbolized "the ingathering of the many new converts from all nations through the disciples' ministry. The gospel net will never break, no matter how many converts it catches."[484] Bultmann agrees that "the net not broken implies the indestructibility of the church—a redactor stress of chapter 21."[485]

I would recommend that those interested in the various opinions of what the number 153 means consult the following authors: Michaels, *The Gospel of John* (pp. 1037–1038); Keener, *The Gospel of John* (pp. 1231–1233); Borchert, *John 12–21* (p. 330); and Carson, *The Gospel According to John* (p. 673). Carson summarizes the various theories by stating, "They tend to offer, at best, an allusion to an admittedly Johannine theme, but nothing that flows naturally out of John 21:11. If the Evangelist has some symbolism in mind connected with the number 153, he has hidden it well."[486] Borchert acknowledges the possibility of the 153 being a symbolic number but then says that "it could, in fact, be an actual reminiscence of an

---

[482] Ibid., 1037.
[483] Blomberg, 276.
[484] Kanagaraj, 208.
[485] Bultmann, 709.
[486] Carson, 673.

event."[487] Perhaps Kostenberger is correct in stating that the number 153 represents simply the number of fish counted and the generous provision of Jesus.[488]

Jesus instructs the disciples to "come and eat breakfast" (21:12), identifying Him as the welcoming host for this fellowship meal. The author inserts for us that none of the disciples "dare ask Him, who are you?" (21:12) At this point in the narrative, the disciples know who the stranger on the shore was: Lord Jesus. Jesus uses the similarity of previous events as the means to reveal Himself to His disciples:

1) He injects conversation to the disciples while they are fishing, similar to Luke 5:4–6. After failing to catch fish, Jesus tells them to try again.
2) In John 21:6 and Luke 5:6, the disciples are obedient to the words of Jesus and reap a harvest of fish.
3) In John 21:7 and Luke 5:8, there is recognition of Jesus, the primary focus in the narrative-based upon 21:1 and 14.
4) The fire of coals in John 18:18 is probably more a reminder for Peter and a setup for his restoration as a true disciple of Jesus.

The question now is whether this large catch of fish qualifies as a miraculous sign in the gospel of John. Several incidents within the narrative push beyond mere coincidences—such as the disciples' obedience to a stranger on the shore approximately one hundred yards away and then enabled to catch 153 large fish without the nets breaking. The fact that the disciple whom Jesus loved was able to recognize Jesus from such a distance, and then the disciple Peter swims that distance to find Jesus with a fire of coals and breakfast ready is above coincidence.

---

[487] Borchert, 330.
[488] Kostenberger, *John*, 593.

Michaels comments that chapter 21 "confirms that there are indeed 'many, and other signs' that Jesus did after his resurrection, signs that the reader should not expect to find 'written in this book' (20:30)."[489] The narrative of the large fishing catch fits Vine's definition of signs as "tokens of divine authority and power."[490] It also fits Roberts's definition of a miracle as "an event that defies common expectations of behavior and subsequently is attributed to a superhuman agent."[491] The impact of the fish is that it became a sign "used by the early Church as a secret Christian insignia as well as a symbol representing Christ and the Eucharist in art and literature. The Greek word Gk. *ichthýs* 'fish' is an acronym whose letters represent *I(ēsous)* Ch (ristos) Th (eou) Y (ios) S (ōtēr), meaning Jesus Christ, Son of God, Savior."[492] Regarding this debatable sign, I believe the large catch of fish qualifies as a miraculous sign pointing us to the deity of Jesus Christ. Let us now move to the ultimate sign of deity, the resurrection of Jesus Christ.

---

[489] Michaels, 1026.

[490] W. E. Vine, *Vine's Complete Expository Dictionary of Old and New Testament Words* (Nashville: Thomas Nelson, 1996), 575.

[491] Roberts, "Miracle," *Lexham Bible Dictionary.*

[492] Myers, 512.

CHAPTER 11

The Ultimate Sign— The Resurrection of Jesus Christ

The resurrection of Jesus is the ultimate miraculous sign presented in the gospel of John and definitively proves the deity of Jesus as the Christ and Son of God. Jesus said in John 2:19 in response to the Jews' request for a sign, "Destroy this temple, and in three days I will raise it up." While the Jews misunderstood and believed He spoke of the temple in Jerusalem, Jesus was prophesying of His death and resurrection. John provides us with his account of the resurrection story, detailing the empty tomb and the witnesses who confirm his bodily resurrection. The Synoptic Gospels each contain their versions of the resurrection story; however, we will focus our attention on John chapter 20 with some references to the other gospels and the writings of Paul.

The Empty Tomb

John's gospel sets the empty tomb scene by informing us that it was the first day of the week, which aligns with Luke 24:1 and particularly Matthew 28:1 and Mark 16:1, which also tells us that it was after the Sabbath. The writer states that Mary Magdalene went to the tomb during the early morning hours while it was still dark. There has been much debate on whether she went alone or made another trip with the other women mentioned in the Synoptic Gospels. I tend to believe that she is mentioned alone in John's gospel because he highlights her role in witnessing the bodily resurrection of Jesus. Carson states that John continues his emphasis on light versus darkness and, in this situation, it is not just the darkness of the hour but the darkness that blankets Mary's understanding.[493]

Mary Magdalene's discovery that the stone has been rolled away (20:1) prompts her to run to Simon Peter and the other disciple whom Jesus loved and inform them of what had happened. Stones were placed over the openings of tombs to protect the bodies from being desecrated by animals; however, in this instance, it was further secured with guards to deter the disciples from stealing the body and claiming that Jesus had risen (Matt. 27:64–65). The fact that the stone had been removed from the entrance, even though it was not easy to move, caused Mary Magdalene to infer that someone had stolen the body of Jesus.[494] Carson states that "the robbing of graves was a crime sufficiently common that Emperor Claudius (41–54 AD) eventually ordered capital punishment to be meted out to those convicted of destroying tombs, removing bodies or even displacing the sealing stones."[495] There is no indication in this narrative that Mary Magdalene attempted to look inside the tomb before going to the disciples. The gospel of Matthew tells us that "an angel of the Lord descended from heaven and came and rolled back the stone from the door and sat on it" (28:2). John's gospel tells us that the stone was taken away (20:1), and the implication is that the body was no longer in the tomb.

---

[493] Carson, 635.
[494] Keener, 1179.
[495] Carson, 636.

The empty tomb is crucial to the foundation of the Christian faith because of its connection to the resurrection of Jesus. Blum argues that "the tomb was open not to let Jesus' body out but to let the disciples and the world see that He rose."[496] There are several rebuttal theories regarding the empty tomb, and I will address only a couple in this project.

1) The women went to the wrong tomb since it was dark. This makes no sense because Jesus was not buried in a public graveyard but in a private burial tomb belonging to Joseph from Arimathea (Matt. 27:57–61). Matthew 27:61 informs us that Mary Magdalene was present at the burial. Are we to believe that she forgot the location of the private grave? After she ran to the disciples, are we to believe that Simon Peter and the disciple whom Jesus loved also went to the wrong grave? Story comments that "John and Peter both saw the empty grave clothes that had been wrapped around Jesus and sealed with spices (John 20:4–6). That can't be accounted for on the wrong-tomb hypothesis."[497] How does the wrong-tomb theory align with Mary Magdalene's encounter with Jesus in the garden? The answer is clearly that she and the disciples were at the empty tomb where Jesus had risen from the dead.

2) Another theory is that the resurrection hoax is based upon hallucination. Of course, the hallucination theory is dependent on all the people who claimed to have seen the empty grave and personally seen Jesus alive being in some state of hallucination. Story again argues that:

> Hallucinations are not contagious. Moreover, people who suffer hallucinations normally do so because they

---

[496] Blum, 342.

[497] D. Story, *Defending Your Faith* (Grand Rapids, MI: Kregel Publications, 1997), 97–98.

want to see something or expect to see something. The disciples were not psychologically prepared to hallucinate because they were not expecting Jesus to rise from the grave. Perhaps the best argument against hallucinations is the fact that on three separate occasions, Jesus was not even recognized (Luke 24:13–31; John 20:15; 21:4). How can you not recognize something you expected or wanted to see badly enough to hallucinate about it?[498]

3) The theory of Jesus's disciple having stolen the body. Matthew's gospel tells us that the tomb was guarded and sealed to prevent Jesus's disciples from stealing the body and claiming that He rose from the grave. The notion that the disciples would steal the body of Jesus seems unbelievable considering John 20:19, which tells us that the disciples were assembled behind closed or locked doors for fear of the Jews. It seems very unlikely that these disciples would have gained the courage to overcome the guards and steal Jesus's body. No one else could gain anything by stealing the body of Jesus and hiding it or reburying it somewhere. There are too many questions regarding the details of such a wild theory to merit further discussion. If someone had stolen the body, then a simple presentation of the body would have disproven the disciples' claim of His resurrection. Foster contends,

> The very state of the grave clothes gave credence to a risen Jesus. They were not in disarray as they would have been left in a furtive act of theft. In fact, if someone were taking the body, why leave the grave clothes at all? The cloth that remained was simply collapsed in the place where the body had been. This in itself was a marvel.[499]

---

[498] Story, 98.
[499] Foster, 310.

Story states, "If the opponents of Christianity could have produced the body of Jesus or any other evidence that He did not rise from the grave, they would have done so."[500] Similarly, Foster advocates,

> From the time of second century Celsus to Hugh Schoenfield's *Passover Plot*, people have been trying unsuccessfully to make a deliberate hoax out of the whole matter. This does not match what Jesus preached and what the disciples continued to preach and live, even to a willingness to die for their testimony. Likewise, the claim of possible confusion of tombs, the suggestion of a spiritual resurrection while Jesus remains decayed in the grave, as well as the various vision and hallucination theories without any physical grounds—all fail woefully to meet the picture unfolded in the Scripture.[501]

I would contend that there is nothing to disprove the historicity of the resurrection of Jesus, and the scene of the empty tomb substantiates the claim. Let us now look at the witnesses to the empty tomb.

Witnesses to the Empty Tomb

John's gospel tells us that Mary Magdalene saw the stone rolled away (20:1); however, it was Peter and the other disciple whom Jesus loved who first actually entered the tomb (20:4–8). Carson comments that the beloved disciple's arrival at the tomb first is merely due to his being younger than Peter and has no symbolic value other than providing details to the resurrection narrative.[502] We are told that the

---

[500] Story, 97.

[501] Foster, 313.

[502] Carson, 637.

beloved disciple looked in and saw the linen cloths but did not enter (20:5). Peter entered the empty tomb first, which fits well with his spontaneous character (18:10). What Peter sees is the linen cloths with which Jesus had previously been wrapped in, and the handkerchief or head wrapping folded separately.

Carson has noted reports of the burial cloths' retaining the shape of Jesus's head and the strips of linen being a proper length for Jesus's body, along with the mixture of spices separating the layers of cloth; however, these reports read more into the text than is actually recorded.[503] We know that the grave clothes were in the tomb along with the handkerchief, which was folded separately from the linen cloths as if to indicate that it was no longer needed. The detailed description of the grave clothes contrasts Jesus's resurrection with Lazarus's. Lazarus needed help to be released from his clothing, whereas Jesus left His behind.[504] Perhaps we should also mention that it is extremely doubtful that grave robbers would have taken the time to remove the linen cloths and fold the handkerchief separately. Our writer clarifies that these two male disciples viewed this scene within the empty tomb. Carson's opinion is that "the description is powerful and vivid, not the sort of thing that would have been dreamed up; and the fact that two men saw it (v. 8) makes their evidence admissible in a Jewish court (Dt. 19:15)."[505]

While outrunning Peter to the tomb, the beloved disciple did not go in but stooped and saw the linen cloths (20:5). After Peter had first witnessed the empty tomb, the beloved disciple went in, saw, and believed (20:8). Our writer does not give Peter's reaction, but he tells us that the beloved disciple saw and believed. Luke 24:12 gives some insight into Peter's seeing, departing, and marveling to himself. We cannot say that Peter came to a confession of faith in response to the resurrection of Jesus. Carson suggests that our best interpretation is

---

[503] Ibid.

[504] Keener, 1182.

[505] Carson, 638.

to conclude that Peter left the tomb wondering about what he saw.[506] The question must be asked concerning the beloved disciple, what did he believe?

Keener advocates that "the beloved disciple becomes the first, hence a paradigmatic believer (20:8), for he believes before a resurrection appearance, merely on the less substantial basis of the empty tomb (cf. 20:29–31)."[507] Keener does, however, acknowledge that the beloved disciple's faith is sign-based and not the ultimate level of faith that is necessary to ascertain the purpose of 20:31.[508] Carson raises the question: If the beloved disciple believed in the resurrection of Jesus, why did he not witness his faith to the other disciples?[509] Michaels suggests that the beloved disciple has a limited faith in that he believed Jesus had gone back to the Father based upon His words in 14:28.[510] In essence, the beloved disciple's faith was based purely on what he saw in the tomb, not on the Scripture regarding Jesus's death and resurrection. Michaels comments further that "true resurrection faith comes to expression in this chapter not when the beloved disciple 'saw and believed,' but only when Mary is able to say, 'I have seen the Lord' (v. 18), and later when the gathered disciples 'rejoiced at seeing the Lord' (v. 20; also v. 25)."[511] I must agree with Carson's and Michaels's opinions that Peter and the beloved disciple did not have full faith in the resurrection of Jesus according to the Scriptures and especially in light of 20:9: "For as yet they did not know the Scriptures that He must rise again from the dead."

Mary Magdalene is the last person our writer identifies as viewing the empty tomb (20:11–12), but what she sees is not the linen cloths but two angels in white sitting at the head and feet of

---

[506] Ibid.
[507] Keener, 1182
[508] Ibid., 1184.
[509] Carson, 639.
[510] Michaels, 992–993.
[511] Ibid.

where the body of Jesus would have been lain (20:13). Our writer does not reconcile the differences between what Peter and the beloved disciple saw versus what Mary Magdalene saw. We will not attempt to indulge in speculations. We can conclude that this scene with the angels communicates the same message as the scattered grave clothes: the body of Jesus is gone, and the angels' presence implies that God was involved in it.[512] In Mary Magdalene's situation at the tomb, she should have realized from the appearance of the angels that Jesus had risen from the dead; however, she continues to cry and hold to the opinion that someone has removed the body. After a mild rebuke by the angels — "Woman, why are weeping?" (20:13)—she saw but did not believe. Michaels states, "Her vision of two angels in white is superior to Peter's vision of scattered grave clothes (v. 6) but it does not generate faith in Jesus' resurrection."[513] More interaction is necessary to awaken her consciousness to the resurrection of Jesus. Let us now address the eyewitnesses of the resurrected Jesus.

Witnesses of the Resurrected Jesus

Mary Magdalene as a Witness

In John 20:14-18, Mary Magdalene is the first to witness the resurrected Jesus and testify to seeing the risen Lord. Jesus is not immediately recognized, as was the case in Luke 24:16 when He walked with the Emmaus disciples. Perhaps Mary Magdalene's eyes were filled with tears, and she was not expecting to see the risen Lord contribute to her not recognizing Jesus. Blum agrees with us that "the appearance of Jesus to Mary was so unexpected that she did not

---

[512] Michaels, 996.
[513] Michaels, 998.

realize that it was Jesus."[514] In a time and culture in which a woman's testimony was considered less valuable than a man's, it is significant that our writer illustrates Mary Magdalene as the first to witness the resurrected Jesus. Blum argues, "No Jewish author in the ancient world would have invented a story with a woman as the first witness to this most important event."[515] Blomberg agrees with Blum:

> An inventor of fiction, trying to commend belief in Jesus's resurrection, would be unlikely to have created women as the first witnesses, much less had focused almost exclusively on one who was formerly demon-possessed (Luke 8:2) and who could therefore be considered out of her mind when she first reported such news (see esp. Byrskog 2000: 75–81).[516]

Kanagaraj reminds us that "for the first-century Christians 'seeing' the risen Jesus was the primary mark of apostolic witness (20:25; cf. 1 Cor. 15:3–9)."[517] There are many speculations on why Mary Magdalene was the first witness of the resurrected Christ, and we will not address them here. The writer makes it definitively clear that Mary Magdalene was the first person to visibly see the resurrected Jesus of Nazareth (20:16–18).

John's gospel informs us that Mary Magdalene does not recognize Jesus (20:14–15) even after Jesus asked her, "Woman, why are you weeping? Whom are you seeking?" She hears the voice of Jesus, but she is so focused on finding where someone has placed His body that she does not recognize His voice and assumes that He is the gardener. What is ironic is that Mary Magdalene is so devoted that she is willing to take the body of Jesus and rebury it (20:15), and what she does not know is that, by offering Himself on the cross,

---

[514] Blum, 342.
[515] Ibid.
[516] Blomberg, 259–260.
[517] Kanagaraj, 197–198.

Jesus has provided the means to take away the sins of the world. It is when Jesus calls her by name (20:16) that she responds, or maybe I should say that she is awakened to the truth of the resurrected Christ or perhaps even that her sight is restored by the power of Jesus's calling her name.

We cannot help but see the practical application of John 10:3–4: "And he calls his own sheep by name and leads them out." Carson comments that "Mary addresses him as she always has: *Rabboni!*—an Aramaic word (cf. notes on 5:2) which John dutifully translates for his Greek-speaking readers (cf. notes on 1:38, 41 and Additional Note)."[518] Michaels notes that the title "Rabbouin, literally 'my Teacher,' is often regarded as a more personal and affectionate title than 'Rabbi,' yet the difference should not be pressed."[519] Perhaps a case could be made that she is a female disciple who has just heard the voice of Jesus, as a Shepherd who calls His sheep.[520] What we can conclude from Mary Magdalene's reaction to hearing Jesus call her name and seeing the resurrected Christ is that she is transformed from despair to delight. This transformation in Mary illustrates Psalm 30:5b: "Weeping may endure for a night, but joy comes in the morning."

We can only imagine the joy and excitement Mary Magdalene must have shown once she realized Jesus had risen from the dead. Her devotion to the dead body of Jesus is shown in the previous verses, and now we can envision her clinging to Jesus like the woman in the parable of Luke 15:8–10 rejoiced after having found a lost silver coin. She wanted to hold onto Him. Jesus's statement in 20:17, "Do not cling to Me, for I have not yet ascended to My Father," has been interpreted numerous ways, and we will not attempt to discuss them in this project. For further enlightenment of this phrase in verse 17,

---

[518] Carson, 641.

[519] Michaels, 999–1000.

[520] Kanagaraj, 197.

I recommend Carson's explanations of four interpretations in *The Gospel According to John* (pp. 642–643).

I see no contradiction between Jesus's telling Mary Magdalene "Do not cling to Me" (20:17) and later extending an invitation to Thomas, saying, "Reach your finger here and look at My hands; and reach your hand here, and put it on My side" (20:27). Michaels notes that "the two situations are not comparable, Mary wants to take hold of Jesus (at least if the analogy with Mt 28:9 is in play) as an act of devotion or worship, while Thomas wants to do so (as we will see) for verification (v. 25)."[521] Mary Magdalene's actions are merely delaying her carrying out the instructions given her (20:17b). Upon hearing Jesus's words, she becomes the first eyewitness, testifying of the resurrected Christ (20:18).

What is interesting to note is that Jesus uses the phrase "My Father and your Father, and My God and your God" in 20:17c. The statement implies a kinship of the disciples due to Jesus's death, resurrection, and exaltation.[522] Michaels agrees that this "pronouncement elevate[s] humankind to the point of being able to address God directly as 'Father,' even as Jesus has done, it confirms at the same time Jesus's humanity, to the point of worshipping 'my God and your God' as any human being might do."[523] Oh, what a wonder to be able to address God with "our Father in heaven, hallowed be Your name" (Matt. 6:9b).

The Disciples as Witnesses

After the resurrection of Jesus, the gospel of John recounts three encounters wherein Jesus reveals Himself to His disciples. The first occurrence in John 20:19–23. We do not know many disciples were present behind the closed or locked doors, but we do know from

---

[521] Michaels, 999–1000.

[522] Carson, 645.

[523] Michaels, 999–1003.

20:24 that Thomas was not present and from Matthew 27:5 that Judas had hanged himself. Kanagaraj contends there is an explicit purpose behind Jesus's showing Himself alive to His disciples:

> The purpose of Jesus's appearance to his disciples is not only to show himself alive (cf. Acts 1:3), but to send them into the world to continue the work of building up his community by witnessing to the truth (18:37), by delivering the world from eternal destruction (3:16–17), and by giving divine life in abundance (10:10).[524]

The gospel of John informs us that it was the evening of the first day of the week, meaning the Sunday when Jesus rose from the dead—what we celebrate as Easter Sunday. I would venture to speculate that the fearful disciples are gathered behind closed or locked doors discussing and contemplating what Peter and the beloved disciple had viewed at the empty tomb (20:5–8). However, since the text is silent on what they were doing, we know they gathered behind those doors out of fear of the Jews. Furthermore, we do not know of the disciples' response to Mary Magdalene's news, but it is reasonable to believe they reacted as Luke records (24:11): "Their words seemed to them like idle tales, and they did not believe them."

The message from Mary Magdalene recorded in 20:18 differs from Matthew 28:7, in which Jesus instructs the disciples to meet Him in Galilee. In contrast, our writer uses this verse (20:18) to set the stage for Jesus's appearance to a group of disciples who are in despair over His death. Kostenberger comments that the disciples are still in Jerusalem due to the Feast of Unleavened Bread and are probably mourning the death of Jesus when Mary Magdalene brings news of seeing the Lord.[525] He provides additional information that "proper residences were equipped with bolts and locks. Bolted doors

---

[524] Kanagaraj, 199.
[525] Kostenberger, *John*, 572.

would prevent anyone from entering (a heavy bolt could be slid through rings attached to the door and its frame) (Keener 1993: 317). Jesus came and stood in the midst."[526]

The situation of the disciples' being in a locked room and then Jesus's appearing suddenly would be understandably frightening. Carson states,

> The function of the locked doors in John's narrative, both here and in v. 26, is to stress the miraculous nature of Jesus' appearance amongst his followers. As his resurrection body passed through the grave-clothes (v. 6–8), so it passed through the locked doors and simply materialized (cf. notes on vv. 14–15).[527]

Jesus greets them with "Peace be with you" (20:19) and begins to show the visible evidence on His hands and His side that He was crucified but has risen from the dead. Kostenberger comments that "Jesus' scars on his hands and his side (cf. 19:34) are marks not only of his suffering but also of his victory (Ridderbos 1995: 64). In fact, his mere presence among his followers is evidence of his triumph (cf. 20:5–7; Moloney 1998: 530–31, 534)."[528]

Our gospel writer does not hesitate to inform us of the reaction of the disciples in 20:20b: "Then the disciples were glad when they saw the Lord." The visible demonstration of the scars of Jesus "became a central confession of the church: the risen Lord is none other than the crucified sacrifice. Temple (p. 366) reminds us that Jesus' wounds are his credentials to the suffering race of human beings."[529] Jesus continues in verses 21–23 to give the commissioning

---

[526] Ibid.
[527] Carson, 646.
[528] Kostenberger, *John*, 572–573.
[529] Carson, 647.

instructions for His disciples to carry out the work that He started on behalf of the Father.

Verses 22 and 23 have generated numerous opinions and perhaps even a foreshadowing of the Day of Pentecost, but we will limit our discussion to the disciples' recognition of the resurrected Jesus. I might inject that the reaction of the disciples to the first group appearance of Jesus does not equate to the reaction of the Holy Spirit on the Day of Pentecost recorded in Acts chapter 2. After this appearance of Jesus to the disciples, another visible appearance occurs eight days later when Thomas is present (20:26). Despite the announcement by Mary Magdalene and the first appearance of Jesus, these disciples are once again behind closed or locked doors, but this time Thomas is present (20:26).

The Disciples' Second Witness of the Resurrected Jesus

The disciple named Thomas, the Twin (*Didymus*) (11:16, 20:24) is often labeled "doubting Thomas" because he makes specific requirements of what he must see to believe Jesus was alive (20:25). Thomas refused to believe despite the other disciples' testimony, "We have seen the Lord" (20:25). Perhaps this second appearance of the resurrected Jesus confirms His resurrection to those who had not physically seen Jesus but were told to believe in Him. Kostenberger comments, "In the present instance, Thomas asks not merely for a sign but for hard evidence. Perhaps he thinks that the disciples actually saw a ghost, not the resurrected Jesus in the flesh (cf. 6:19–21 pars.)."[530] Thomas's doubt or skepticism in his fellow disciples indicates what ministers of the gospel face today in that many people will not believe our testimony because they have not seen Jesus for themselves.

---

[530] Kostenberger, *John*, 578.

Thomas's objection to the resurrection of Jesus in the flesh feeds the notion "that Jesus only appeared to be human (the heresy later termed 'Docetism'")[531] Spong holds the opinion that "God has raised Jesus to new life, but nowhere does that mean resuscitation back into the life of this world. Jesus was raised into the life of God and made universally available. He was not resuscitated to walk again the dark streets of Jerusalem or the dusty trails of Galilee."[532] Keener argues to the contrary:

> Within earliest Christianity, however, there remains no debate about the received tradition that Jesus himself rose bodily, unless one is inclined to count inferences by some modern scholars without explicit supporting evidence. By some point in the second century, however, gnostics and others who found the notion of a bodily resurrection of any sort incompatible with Platonic metaphysics sought to interpret the early Christian tradition differently (cf. e.g., in Irenaeus *Haer.* 2.29).[533]

Our writer of the gospel in this narrative of John 20:24–29 is making a case for the bodily resurrection of Jesus instead of some hallucination or ghostly occurrence. On a Sunday, Jesus comes to the disciples when they are once again behind closed or locked doors and greets them by saying, "Peace to you" (20:26).[534] Jesus immediately demonstrates His divine ability to hear and know their conversations without being physically present. Thomas is specifically challenged in 20:27 to examine the physical, hard evidence of the resurrected Jesus who is standing in their midst. What I find interesting in this narrative is that we are not told that Thomas takes Jesus up

---

[531] Ibid.
[532] Spong, 266.
[533] Keener, 1177.
[534] Carson, 657.

on His offer to examine Him. Carson argues that the sight of Jesus Himself proved sufficient (v. 29) to Thomas, who was astounded with reverence to the point of voicing his confession.[535] Kostenberger agrees, saying, "Rather, in a peak (at least) akin to the recognition scene in 20:16, Thomas acknowledges Jesus as his Lord and God."[536] I also align with Kostenberger's opinion that Thomas's expression of "my Lord and my God" (20:28) is a climactic confession that connects the deity of Jesus to the Word made flesh in 1:1, 14, and 18.[537]

Again, our gospel writer is making a case for full belief in the crucified and now resurrected Jesus. Keener comments,

> Not all streams of early Judaism clearly articulate a doctrine of bodily resurrection. The Sadducees denied it (Josephus Ant. 18.16–17; War 2.165); rabbinic texts, which here probably represent the populist Pharisaic consensus, complain about the offensiveness of such a denial. The Qumran community likely supported bodily resurrection.[538]

Jesus responds to Thomas in 20:29, but it is also a universal response to those who base their faith on "seeing and believing" instead of believing by faith in the resurrected Jesus. It is, as Kostenberger suggests, a mild rebuke to those who base their faith on what they can see.[539] As a reminder, the story of the resurrected Jesus Christ is recorded in all four Gospels (Matt. 28:1–20; Mark 16:1–8; Luke 24:1 53; John 20:1–21:25). A third appearance of the resurrected Jesus to the disciples occurs in John 21, and we have discussed this scripture passage in chapter 10, "Debatable Signs." I

---

[535] Ibid.
[536] Kostenberger, *John*, 579.
[537] Ibid.
[538] Keener, 1176.
[539] Kostenberger, *John*, 580.

believe the purpose of the gospel is satisfied in prompting the reader to believe that Jesus is the Christ, the Son of God. Consider now a few scriptural witnesses outside of the gospel writings.

Other Witnesses of the Resurrected Jesus

Grudem tells us that "the book of Acts is a story of the apostles' proclamation of the resurrection of Christ, and of continued prayer to Christ and trust in Him as the one who is alive and reigning in heaven."[540] Specifically, we are told of Stephen's confession while being stoned of seeing "the Son of Man standing at the right hand of God" (Acts 7:56). In his prayer to God, while being stoned, he prayed, "Lord Jesus, receive my spirit" (Acts 7:59). We must conclude that Stephen while being stoned, was an eyewitness of the resurrected Christ. Furthermore, there is the story of Saul's conversion as he traveled on the road to Damascus to persecute the church in Acts 9. While Saul/Paul acknowledges hearing the voice of Jesus (Acts 9:4, 22:7, 26:14), we must include him as a witness of the resurrected Jesus Christ.

Grudem adds that Paul's writing in "the Epistles depend[s] entirely on the assumption that Jesus is a living, reigning Savior who is now exalted head of the church, who is to be trusted, worshipped, and adored, and who will someday return in power and great glory to reign as King over the earth."[541] Paul's writing in 1 Corinthians 15:3–9 documents the numerous people who witnessed the resurrected Jesus, including over five hundred brethren at one particular time. In 1 Corinthians 15:8, Paul writes, "Then last of all He was seen by me also, as by one born out of due time." Garland comments, "Paul confidently includes the risen Christ's appearance to him in the roll call of eyewitnesses even though it occurred at some distance in the

---

[540] Wayne Grudem, *Bible Doctrine: Essential Teachings of the Christian Faith* (Grand Rapids, MI: Zondervan, 1999), 261

[541] Grudem, 261.

time from the other appearances and no one else could corroborate this account."[542]

I conclude this section by advocating that Stephen and Paul were eyewitnesses to the resurrected Jesus Christ. Perhaps we could even make the case in support of Garland that Paul (based on 1 Cor. 15:8) was the last eyewitnesses of the resurrected Christ. "Others may have visions of Christ, but they are not on the same level as the appearances of the resurrected Christ to the apostles."[543] The Scriptures within the gospel of John, Acts, and 1 Corinthians all provide sufficient eyewitnesses that Jesus is the Christ, Son of God. I want to conclude chapter 11 with a few comments arguing that the resurrection of Jesus Christ is the ultimate proof of His deity.

The Resurrection of Christ Is the Ultimate Proof that Jesus Is the Son of God

The resurrected Jesus is a pillar in the foundation of the Christian faith that demonstrated Jesus Christ's power over sin and death. Cook agrees with me:

> The bodily resurrection of Jesus is one of the central tenets of the Christian faith. His bodily resurrection validates the claim that He is both Lord and Christ. It substantiates the proposition that His life and death were not just the life and death of a good man but that He indeed was God incarnate and that by His death, we have forgiveness of sin.[544]

---

[542] David E. Garland, *1 Corinthians: Baker Exegetical Commentary on the New Testament* (Grand Rapids, MI: Baker Academic, 2003), 690.

[543] Ibid., 691.

[544] B. Cook, "Resurrection of Jesus the Christ," *Holman Illustrated Bible Dictionary* (Nashville: Holman Bible Publishers, 2003), 1381.

Hodge states, "If Christ did not rise, the whole scheme of redemption is a failure, and all the predictions and anticipations of its glorious results for time and eternity, for men and for angels of every rank and order, are proved to be chimeras."[545] Hagner writes that the fear of the Jewish leaders in Matthew 27:64, "He has risen from the dead," became a reality and "the central element of the church's kerygma."[546]

Paul writes in 1 Corinthians 15:13-14, "But if there be no resurrection of the dead, then is Christ not risen. And if Christ be not risen, then is our preaching vain, and your faith is also vain." In essence, the payment for sin was completely satisfied, and the wrath of God was appeased, as evidenced by the resurrected body of Jesus Christ, who would never die again. Duffield contends that "it was His resurrection which demonstrated that He was the Son of God. His resurrection proves that His death was of sufficient value to God to cover all our sins, for His sacrifice was the sacrifice of the Son of God."[547] The resurrection of Jesus Christ is the ultimate sign of His being the Son of God.

N. T. Wright contends that the verses of 1 Corinthians 15:1–3 are part of a foundation story in which the community did not tamper with but passed this information down to other believers, followers of the way, without altering the original story. If this concept is true, we must agree that eyewitness believers testified to the resurrection act in that they saw the risen Christ Jesus after the crucifixion. Wright comments,

---

[545] Charles Hodge, *Systematic Theology*, vol. 2 of Anthropology (Peabody, MA: Hendrickson, 2008), 627.

[546] Donald A. Hagner, *Word Biblical Commentary, Matthew*, vol. 33b (Dallas: Thomas Nelson, Inc., 1995), 862.

[547] G. P. Duffield, and N. M. Van Cleave, *Foundations of Pentecostal Theology* (Los Angeles, CA: L.I.F.E. Bible College, 1983), 193.

The earliest Christians believed both that Jesus had been bodily raised and that this even fulfilled the scriptural stories. These were perceived as stories not simply about a Messiah emerging out of the blue, but about Israel, about the doing away with Israel's time of desolation, about the coming of the new age that would reverse the effects of the present evil age.[548]

I agree with the predominant Scriptures within the Gospels and the other New Testament writings identifying multiple witnesses of the bodily resurrection of Jesus Christ as the ultimate proof of His being the Son of God.

---

[548] N. T. Wright, *The Resurrection of the Son of God* (Minneapolis: Fortress Press, 2003), 322.

CHAPTER 12

Final Conclusions

As I draw this project to a conclusion, several questions mandate a response to whether the miraculous signs within the gospel of John provide definitive proof of the deity of Jesus Christ.

Whether These Miraculous Signs Individually or Collectively Support the Deity of Jesus Christ

Our definition of *signs* presented in the glossary argues that miracles are visible tokens and indicators of the identity of Jesus Christ, the Son of God. We must keep in mind that all the miraculous signs were not performed for the general audience, and in fact, most of them were aimed at a specific individual or group of people. For example, the changing of water into wine was enjoyed by those attending the wedding in Cana, but John's gospel tells us that the miracle "manifested His glory; and His disciples believed in Him" (2:11). The case could be made that this miracle benefited those present, but the impact of being a visible token of the deity of Jesus Christ was grasped only by the disciples. The healing of the nobleman's son;

whereas other people probably heard the conversation between Jesus and the nobleman, the impact of the healing was attested to by the nobleman, his servants, and his household. The writer informs us that "he himself believed, and his whole household" (4:53). John's gospel does not tell us specifically what the disciples or the nobleman believed; however, we cannot help but assume based on 20:31 that these people possessed faith in Jesus Christ.

Various individuals or groups' belief in Jesus Christ does not necessarily mean that they had acquired full faith in the resurrected Jesus Christ as the Son of God. John's gospel repeatedly informs us of the Jews' and the disciples' misunderstanding of Jesus's words and drawing a conclusion short of the deity of Jesus. In John 6:14, after the feeding of the five thousand, the men stated, "This is truly the Prophet who is to come into the world." Then later in the same chapter, after Jesus spoke of eating His flesh and drinking His blood, the writer tells us that "many of His disciples, when they heard this, said, this is a hard saying: who can understand it" (6:60). Jesus acknowledges their doubt, saying, "There are some of you who do not believe" (6:64), which lets us know that the miracle of feeding the five thousand did not persuade the multitude to believe Jesus is the Christ, Son of God.

Simon Peter, however, confesses in verse 69, "We have come to believe and know that You are the Christ, the Son of the living God." Perhaps we could make the case that because the disciples distributed the bread and fish to the multitude (6:11), they knew Jesus had supernaturally multiplied the lad's five barley loaves and two small fish (6:9). So, while some people doubted Jesus even after the miraculous sign, others believed in alignment with the purpose expressed in 20:31. All who witnessed the miraculous signs did not believe immediately. Still, I suspect John's gospel is written in an aftermath format for the reader to conclude his purpose in 20:31. Brown argues,

In John, a sign refers to a miracle of Jesus in the present time, which testifies to his messiahship. In the Synoptic, miracles demonstrate the presence of the kingdom of God (Matthew 12:28). In the Gospel of John, they point to the nature of Jesus. They are signs, however, only to men of faith (12:37). They also testify to the power and glory of God and are realizations in part of his salvation, which has appeared in the messianic age.[549]

It is debatable whether each miraculous sign individually provides definitive proof of the deity of Jesus Christ. Still, when combined as a collective gospel, they are more than sufficient in revealing token symbols of the deity of Jesus. I believe that each sign has a particular message as a token of the deity of Jesus. Consider the following: turning water to wine symbolizes His power over quality; healing the nobleman's son symbolizes His power over a distance; healing the impotent man symbolizes His power over time; feeding the five thousand symbolizes His power over quantity; walking on water symbolizes His power over natural law; healing the blind man shows His power over helplessness, and raising Lazarus from the dead shows His power over death.[550] All of these miracles are unparalleled and unique to the ministry of Jesus. In our prior discussion of the traditional seven signs, we stressed that only someone with divine power and authority could perform these miracles.

Let us revisit these signs briefly for a moment.

1) The master of the feast verified the transformation of water to wine, and the writer informs us that the servants knew where it had come from (2:9). There was nothing added to the waterpots because they were filled to the brim (2:7). The water was miraculously changed somewhere between filled

---

[549] Brown, "The Distinctives of John's Gospel," 31.
[550] Reginald H. Fuller, *Interpreting the Miracles* (London: SCM, 1963).

pots and the servants' drawing wine out. Other "miracles" that suggest a change in liquid are accomplished by adding some type of ingredient. This miracle points us to the deity of Jesus Christ.

2) The nobleman and his servants verified the healing of the nobleman's son. The healing occurred at the same hour in which Jesus spoke the words, "Go your way; your son lives" (4:50, 53). There is no reason to believe that the nobleman's son was healed by any other means. There are no other accounts of healing that compare to Jesus's healing of this man's son over approximately fifteen miles with the spoken word. This miracle points us to the deity of Jesus Christ.

3) The healing of the impotent man at the pool of Bethesda was unique in that the man had been sick for over thirty-eight years. Jesus again uses the power of His spoken word to heal a man who frankly did not demonstrate faith. It was a supernatural demonstration of the sovereignty of our Lord Jesus to heal this man, especially on the Sabbath day. This miracle points us to Jesus's divine power and the fact that He is Lord of the Sabbath day.

4) The feeding of the five thousand with five barley loaves and two small fish manifests the deity of Jesus to utilize humankind's limited resources and generate a superabundance for needy people.

5) Jesus's walking on the Sea of Galilee is unequaled in historical records and shows His divine power over the sea, which can symbolize the chaos in our lives.

6) Jesus's healing of the man born blind demonstrates His power to resolve physical and spiritual conditions that have postured us in a helpless state from birth. I would argue that Jesus used His divine creative power to grant eyesight to the man born blind, and there is no other historical account of such a miracle.

7) When Jesus raised Lazarus from the dead, it placed this miraculous sign beyond the level of resuscitation. Lazarus had been dead for four days, plus the body had started to decay, which according to Jewish beliefs, meant the spirit had left him. This miraculous sign ties directly with John 1:4: "In Him was life, and the life was the light of men." The ultimate sign of deity is the resurrection of Jesus from the grave and His resurrection being witnessed by many people. I would argue that there is sufficient evidence within these individual signs to point us to the deity of Jesus Christ, so let us consider the second question.

Whether There Is Sufficient Evidence for the Audience to Have Faith in Jesus Christ as the Son of God

I believe John is advocating sufficient evidence for the audience to believe in Jesus, whether it is composed of Jews or Gentiles. In essence, we would contend that our writer hand-picked these particular miraculous signs based upon 20:30 with the purpose mentioned in 20:31. All of the miraculous signs show an individual or a group of people grasping the supernatural impact of what was performed by Jesus. Despite the audience's preconceived understanding of social, religious, and even theological concepts, the miraculous signs consistently stand out as tokens of divine intervention. The gospel of John reflects a willful rejection of Jesus despite the miraculous signs. For example, after Jesus healed the man at the pool of Bethesda on the Sabbath day, we are informed that "for this reason the Jews persecuted Jesus, and sought to kill Him, because He had done these things on the Sabbath" (5:16). Likewise, after the resurrection of Lazarus, the gospel writer tells us, "Then, from that day on, they plotted to put Him to death" (11:53). The restoration of life to a dead corpus should indicate divine intervention; however, the chief priest and Pharisees willfully reject Jesus. They are willing to plot

Jesus's death instead of accepting life. This reminds us of the choice of Adam and Eve in the Garden of Eden; in essence, by eating from the tree of the knowledge of good and evil, they chose death instead of life.

Perhaps more research is warranted into the debatable signs, specifically the audience impact of Jesus's cleansing the temple as a miraculous sign of His divine authority. Bauckham expresses the view that "the great catch of fish in chapter 21 is not a sign in this Johannine sense, but a miracle with a quite different purpose. It symbolizes programmatically the mission in which the disciples are now to engage."[551]

The early church movement and the current-day Christian movement are predicated on the resurrection of Jesus Christ. The disciples' boldness due to the promised Holy Spirit is directly linked to Jesus's rising from the dead and commissioning them as witnesses. Paul writes in 1 Corinthians 15:14, "And if Christ is not risen, then our preaching is empty, and your faith is also empty." I believe there is more than enough evidence documented in these miracle narratives for the immediate audience and the current-day audience to believe Jesus is the Christ, Son of God.

---

[551] Richard Bauckham, *The Testimony of the Beloved Disciple, Narrative, History, and Theology in the Gospel of John* (Grand Rapids, MI: Baker Academic, 2007), 274.

GLOSSARY

Jews: According to Vine's, the word *Jews*, which is used most frequently in the gospel of John and the Acts, "denotes the typical representatives of Jewish thought contrasted with believers in Christ ... or with other Jews of less pronounced opinions."[552] Culpepper contends that the term *Jews* as used in "the Johannine use of the term has no nationalistic meaning since it distinguishes 'Jews' from others of the same national, religious, cultural group and designates a group with a constant, unchanging hostility toward Jesus."[553] In various chapters of John's narratives of the signs, the term *Jews* can refer to different groups, but they are all related to the spiritual group that opposes Jesus. In the discourse in John 6:48, wherein Jesus said, "I am the bread of life," Smith claims that the term *Jews* (*Ioudaioi*) is more than simply Judeans or residents of Judea but inclusive of "people who on religious ground are opposed to Jesus."[554] "In Romans 2:17–29 Paul gives an interesting theological analysis of the term 'Jew.' He is at pains to emphasize that the true meaning of the word lies not in the outward religious profession but an inward attitude to God."[555]

---

[552] Vine, 334.

[553] Culpepper, *Anatomy of the Fourth Gospel*, 126.

[554] Smith, 30.

[555] Elwell and Beitzel, "Jew," *Baker Encyclopedia of the Bible*, 1164–1165.

Therefore, in this project, we ignore the nationalistic meaning of the term *Jews* and use the term *Jew* to specifically identify the group of people within the Jewish race who were in opposition to Jesus.

Miracles: A strong and perhaps identical relationship exists between the definitions of *miracles* and *signs*. Myers describes a miracle as "an event remarkable in that it goes contrary to the laws of nature, that is, to the usual course of events."[556] Roberts explains a miracle as "an event that defies common expectations of behavior and subsequently is attributed to a superhuman agent; an occurrence that demonstrates God's involvement in the course of human affairs."[557] Roberts's definition of *miracles* links them with divine intervention. Grudem states, "A miracle is a less common kind of God's activity in which he arouses people's awe and wonder and bears witness to himself."[558] For this study, we will propose that the miracles by the above definitions are signs authenticating and conveying the meaning of divine authority, or in other words, the miracles in John's gospel are signs due to the significant relationship of the miracle as opposed to the marvel of the event itself.

Signs: There are numerous definitions of *signs,* and we will consider several in formulating our definition. Vine defines signs as "tokens of divine authority and power,"[559] whereas Strong describes signs as "a mark to indicate or signify."[560] Baker describes signs as "connoting a visible event intended to convey meaning beyond that which is normally perceived in the outward appearance of the event."[561] At

---

[556] Myers, *Eerdmans Bible Dictionary*, 722.

[557] R. D. Roberts, "Miracle," *Lexham Bible Dictionary* (Bellingham, WA: Lexham Press, 2016).

[558] Grudem, *Systematic Theology*, 355.

[559] Vine, 575.

[560] James Strong, *The New Strong's Exhaustive Concordance of the Bible* (Nashville: Thomas Nelson, 1990), 65.

[561] Elwell and Beitzel, *Baker Encyclopedia of the Bible*, Vol. 2, 1961.

the same time, Kostenberger classifies them as being more than just miracles. He claims that the significance is not in the sign itself but that it points us to the fact that Jesus is the Christ and Son of God.[562] This study will suggest an integration of these definitions and contend that signs are miracles in that they are visible tokens and indicators of the identity of Jesus Christ, the Son of God.

---

[562] Kostenberger, *Encountering John*, 23.

BIBLIOGRAPHY

Ainslie, Peter. "Among the Gospels and the Acts Being Notes and Comments Covering the Life of Christ in the Flesh, and the First Thirty Years' History of His Church." Baltimore: Temple Seminary Press, 1908, 234–235.

Ashby, Godfrey William. "Body and Blood in John 6:41–65." *Neotestamentica* 36, nos. 1–2 (2002): 59.

Barrett, Charles K. *The Gospel According to John: An Introduction with Commentary and Notes on the Greek Text.* Philadelphia: The Westminster Press, 1978.

Bauckham, Richard. *Jesus and the Eyewitnesses: The Gospels as Eyewitness Testimony.* Grand Rapids, MI: Eerdmans Publishing, 2006.

Bauckham, Richard. *The Testimony of the Beloved Disciple: Narrative, History, and Theology in the Gospel of John.* Grand Rapids, MI: Baker Academic, 2007.

Blomberg, Craig L. *The Historical Reliability of John's Gospel: Issues and Commentary.* Downers Grove, IL: Inter Varsity Press, 2001.

Blum, Edwin A. "John." In *The Bible Knowledge Commentary: An Exposition of the Scriptures,* eds. John F. Walvoord and Roy B. Zuck. Vol. 2. Wheaton, IL: Victor Books, 1985.

Borchert, Gerald L. *John 1–11.* Vol. 25A. Nashville: Broadman and Holman Publishers, 1996.

Brown, Raymond E. "The Distinctives of John's Gospel." *Southwestern Journal of Theology* 8, no. 1 (Oct. 1965): 25–34.

Brown, Raymond E. *The Gospel and Epistles of John: A Concise Commentary.* Collegeville, MI: Liturgical Press, 1988.

Brown, Sherri. "Water Imagery and the Power and Presence of God in the Gospel of John." *Theology Today* 72 (2015): 289–298.

Bryan, Steven M. "Power in the Pool: The Healing of the Man at Bethesda and Jesus' Violation of the Sabbath." *Tyndale Bulletin* 54.2 (2003): 8.

Bultmann, Rudolf. *The Gospel of John: A Commentary,* trans. G. R. Beasley-Murrary. Philadelphia: Westminster Press, 1971.

Carson, Donald A. *The Gospel According to John.* Grand Rapids, MI: Eerdmans Publishing Company, 1991.

Carver, Amanda Cookson. "Galilee, Sea of, Archaeology of." In *The Lexham Bible Dictionary,* eds. John D. Barry, David Bomar, Derek R. Brown, Rachel Klippenstein, Douglas Mangum, Carrie Sinclair Wolcott, ... Wendy Widder. Bellingham, WA: Lexham Press, 2016.

Cook, Bill. "Resurrection of Jesus the Christ." In *Holman Illustrated Bible Dictionary.* Nashville: Holman Bible Publishers, 2003.

Culpepper, R. Alan. *Anatomy of the Fourth Gospel: A Study in Literary Design.* Philadelphia: Fortress, 1983.

———. "Cognition in John: The Johannine Signs as Recognition Scenes." *Perspective in Religious Studies* 35, no. 3 (2008): 251–260.

———. *The Gospel and Letters of John.* Nashville: Abingdon Press, 1988.

Culpepper, R. Alan, and C. Clifton Black. *Exploring the Gospel of John.* Louisville, KY: Westminster John Knox Press, 1996.

Deere, Jack S. "Song of Songs." In *The Bible Knowledge Commentary: An Exposition of the Scriptures,* vol. 1, eds. John F. Walvoord and Roy B. Zuck. Wheaton, IL: Victor Books, 1985.

D. T. "Health, Disease and Healing." In *New Bible Dictionary,* 3rd ed. Eds. D. R. W. Wood, Ian Howard Marshall, Alan Ralph

Millard, James Innell Packer, and Donald John Wiseman. Downers Grove, IL: InterVarsity Press, 1996.

Duffield, Guy P., and Nathaniel M. Van Cleave. *Foundations of Pentecostal Theology*. Los Angeles: L.I.F.E. Bible College, 1983.

Dunnett, Walter M. *Exploring the New Testament*. Wheaton, IL: Crossway Books, 2001.

Easton, Matthew George. "Nobleman." In *Easton's Bible Dictionary*. New York: Harper and Brothers, 1893.

Edersheim, Alfred. *The Temple, Its Ministry and Services as They Were at the Time of Jesus Christ*. London: James Clarke and Co., 1959.

———. *The Life and Times of Jesus the Messiah*. Vol. 1. New York: Longmans, Green, and Co., 1896.

———. *Sketches of Jewish Social Life in the Days of Christ*. London: The Religious Tract Society, n.d.

Edwards, James R. *Discovering John*. London: Society for Promoting Christian Knowledge, 2003.

Elowsky, Joel C. *Ancient Christian Commentary on Scripture, New Testament IVa John 1–10*. Downers Grove, IL: InterVarsity Press, 2006.

Elwell, Walter A. and Barry J. Beitzel. *Baker Encyclopedia of the Bible*. Vols. 1–2. Grand Rapids, MI: Baker Book House, 1988.

Erickson, Millard, J. *Christian Theology*, 3rd ed. Grand Rapids, MI: Baker Academic, 2013.

Farrer, Austin. *A Study in St. Mark*. Westminster: Dacre Press, 1951.

Foster, Louis. *John: Unlocking the Scriptures for You*. Cincinnati: Standard, 1987.

Fredriksen, Paula. *Jesus of Nazareth, King of the Jews*: *A Jewish Life and the Emergence of Christianity*. New York: Alfred A. Knopf, 1999.

Fuller, Reginald H. *Interpreting the Miracles*. London: SCM, 1963.

Fullilove, William B. "Bethany Beyond the Jordan." In *The Lexham Bible Dictionary*, eds. by John D. Barry, David Bomar, Derek R. Brown, Rachel Klippenstein, Douglas Mangum, Carrie Sinclair

Wolcott, … Wendy Widder. Bellingham, WA: Lexham Press, 2016.

Gangel, Kenneth O. *John*. Vol. 4. Nashville: Broadman and Holman Publishers, 2000.

Garland, David E. *1 Corinthians: Baker Exegetical Commentary on the New Testament*. Grand Rapids, MI: Baker Academic, 2003.

Geddert, Timothy J. *Mark*. Scottdale, PA: Herald Press, 2001.

Geisler, Norman L. "The Bible Does Not Teach that New Testament Communion Wine Was Unfermented." *Bibliotheca sacra* 139, no. 553 (January–March 1982): 46–56.

Gromacki, Robert G. *New Testament Survey*. Grand Rapids, MI: Baker Academic, 1974.

Grudem, Wayne. *Bible Doctrine: Essential Teachings of the Christian Faith*. Grand Rapids, MI: Zondervan, 1999.

Grudem, Wayne. *Systematic Theology: An Introduction to Biblical Doctrine*. Grand Rapids, MI: Zondervan Publishing House, 1994.

Guyer, Michael S. "Bethany on the Mount of Olives." In *The Lexham Bible Dictionary*, eds. John D. Barry, David Bomar, Derek R. Brown, Rachel Klippenstein, Douglas Mangum, Carrie Sinclair Wolcott, … Wendy Widder. Bellingham, WA: Lexham Press, 2016.

Hagner, Donald A. *Word Biblical Commentary. Matthew,* vol. 33b. Dallas: Thomas Nelson, Inc., 1995.

Hahn, Roger L. *Matthew: A Commentary for Bible Students*. Indianapolis: Wesleyan Publishing House, 2007.

Harvey, Anthony Ernest. *The Journal of Theological Studies*. Vol. 54, no 2. Publication Type: Review, 2003.

Hodge, Charles. *Systematic Theology*. Vol. 1. "Theology." Peabody, MA: Hendrickson Publishers, 2008.

Hodge, Charles. *Systematic Theology*. Vol. 2. "Anthropology." Peabody, MA: Hendrickson Publishers, 2008.

Holman Illustrated Bible Dictionary. Chad Brand, Charles Draper, Archie England, Steve Bond, E. Ray Clendenen, and Trent

C. Butler, eds. s.v. "Sheep Gate." Nashville: Holman Bible Publishers, 2003.

Horst, Pieter W van der. "Review of Aus, Roger D., *Feeding the Five Thousand*: Studies in the Judaic Background of Mark 6:30–44 par. and John 6:1–15." *Novum testamentum* 53, no. 4. Lanham, MD: University Press of America, 2010, 405–406.

Hughes, R. Kent. *John: That You May Believe*. Wheaton, IL: Crossway Books, 1999.

Jamieson, Robert, Andrew R. Fausset, and David Brown. *Commentary Critical and Explanatory on the Whole Bible*. Vol. 2. Oak Harbor, WA: Logos Research Systems, Inc., 1997.

Kanagaraj, Jey J. *John, A New Covenant Commentary*. Eugene, OR: Cascade Books, 2013.

Keener, Craig, S. *The Gospel of John: A Commentary*. Vol.1. Grand Rapids, MI: Baker Academic, 2003.

Kendall, Robert T. *Understanding Theology*. Vol. 2. Ross-shire, Great Britain: Christian Focus, 2000.

Klinger, Jerzy. "Bethesda and the Universality of the Logos." *St. Vladimir's Theological Quarterly* 27, no. 3 (1983): 169–185.

Knight, George William. "Capernaum." In *Holman Illustrated Bible Dictionary*, eds. Chad Brand, Charles Draper, Archie England, Steve Bond, E. Ray Clendenen, and Trent C. Butler. Nashville: Holman Bible Publishers, 2003.

Knowles, Andrew. *The Bible Guide*. 1st Augsburg Books ed. Minneapolis: Augsburg, 2001.

Kobia, Samuel. "What's in a Miracle? Feeding the Five Thousand." *The Ecumenical Review* 59, no. 4 (October 2007): 534.

Koester, Craig R. *Symbolism in the Fourth Gospel: Meaning, Mystery, Community*. Minneapolis: Fortress, 1995.

Kostenberger, Andreas J. *Encountering John: The Gospel in Historical, Literary, and Theological Perspective*. Grand Rapids, MI: Baker Academic, 2013.

Kostenberger, Andreas J. *John: Baker Exegetical Commentary on the New Testament*. Grand Rapids, MI: Baker Academic, 2004.

Kysar, Robert. *Preaching John*. Minneapolis: Fortress Press, 2002.

Laney, J. Carl. "Galilee." In *The Lexham Bible Dictionary*, eds. John D. Barry, David Bomar, Derek R. Brown, Rachel Klippenstein, Douglas Mangum, Carrie Sinclair Wolcott, ... Wendy Widder. Bellingham, WA: Lexham Press, 2016.

Lange, John Peter and Phillip Schaff. *A Commentary on the Holy Scriptures: John*. Bellingham, WA: Logos Bible Software, 2008.

Latourelle, Rene. *The Miracles of Jesus and the Theology of Miracles*, trans. Matthew J. O'Connell. Mahwah, NJ: Paulist Press, 1988.

Leavell, Landrum P. "Mark." In *The Teacher's Bible Commentary*, eds. H. F. Paschall and H. H. Hobbs. Nashville: Broadman and Holman Publishers, 1972.

Lenski, Richard Charles Henry. *The Interpretation of St. John's Gospel*. Minneapolis: Augsburg Publishing House, 1961.

Lincoln, Andrew T. *The Gospel According to Saint John*. London: Continuum, 2005.

Lockyer, Herbert. *All the Men of the Bible*. Grand Rapids, MI: Zondervan Publishing House, 1958.

Lockyer, Herbert, R.S.L. *All the Women of the Bible*. Grand Rapids, MI: Zondervan Publishing House.

Lohse, Eduard, and Georg Fohrer. "Σιών, Ἰερουσαλήμ, Ἰεροσόλυμα, Ἰεροσολυμίτης." In *Theological Dictionary of the New Testament*, eds. Gerhard Kittel, Geoffrey W. Bromiley, and Gess Friedrich. Electronic ed., vol. 7. Grand Rapids, MI: Eerdmans, 1964.

MacArthur, John. *Twelve Extraordinary Women: How God Shaped Women of the Bible, and What He Wants to Do with You*. Nashville: Thomas Nelson Publishers, 2005.

Malina, Bruce J., and Richard L. Rohrbaugh. *Social-Science Commentary on the Gospel of John*. Minneapolis: Fortress Press, 1998.

McFadyen, Phillip. *Open Door on John: A Gospel for Our Time*. London: Triangle, 1998.

McGarvey, John William, and Phillip Y. Pendleton. *The Four-Fold Gospel*. Cincinnati: The Standard Publishing Company, 1914.

McPhee, Brian D. "Walk, Don't Run: Jesus's Water Walking Is Unparalleled in Greco-Roman Mythology." *Journal of Biblical Literature* 135, no. 4 (2016).

McReynolds, Paul R. *Mark: Unlocking the Scriptures for You.* Cincinnati: Standard, 1989.

Michaels, J. Ramsey. *The Gospel of John: The New International Commentary on the New Testament.* Grand Rapids, MI: Eerdmans Publishing Company, 2010.

Michaels, J. Ramsey, and W. Ward Gasque. *John: New International Commentary.* Peabody, MA: Hendrickson Publishers, 1989.

Miller, Jeffrey E. "Cana of Galilee." In *The Lexham Bible Dictionary,* eds. John D. Barry, David Bomar, Derek R. Brown, Rachel Klippenstein, Douglas Mangum, Carrie Sinclair Wolcott, ... Wendy Widder. Bellingham, WA: Lexham Press, 2016.

Moloney, Francis J. S.D.B. *The Gospel of John,* Sacra Pagina Series, Vol.4. Collegeville, MI: The Liturgical Press, 2005.

Myers, Allen C. *Eerdmans Bible Dictionary.* Grand Rapids, MI: Eerdmans, 1987.

Newman, Barclay M. and Eugene A. Nida. *A Handbook on the Gospel of John.* New York: United Bible Societies, 1993.

Neyrey, Jerome. *The Gospel of John.* New York: Cambridge University Press, 2007.

O'Day, Gail R., and Susan E. Hylen. *John.* Louisville, KY: Westminster John Knox Press, 2006.

Powell, Mark Allan. "Zurishaddai." In *The HarperCollins Bible Dictionary,* 3rd ed. New York: HarperCollins, 2011.

Redford, Douglas. *The Life and Ministry of Jesus: The Gospels,* Vol. 1. Cincinnati: Standard Pub., 2007.

Richardson, Alan. "The Feeding of the Five Thousand: Mark 6:34–44." *Interpretation* 9, no. 2 (Apr. 1955): 144–149.

Riggans, Walter. "The Jewish Reclamation of Jesus and Its Implications for Jewish-Christian Relations." *Themelios* 18, no. 1 (1992): 10.

Roberts, Ronald D. "Miracle" In *Lexham Bible Dictionary,* eds. John D. Barry, David Bomar, Derek R. Brown, Rachel Klippenstein, Douglas Mangum, Carrie Sinclair Wolcott, ... Wendy Widder. Bellingham, WA: Lexham Press, 2016.

Rosscup, James E. *An Exposition on Prayer in the Bible: Igniting the Fuel to Flame Our Communication with God.* Bellingham, WA: Lexham Press, 2008.

Ryan, Jordan. "Tiberias." In *The Lexham Bible Dictionary,* eds. John D. Barry, David Bomar, Derek R. Brown, Rachel Klippenstein, Douglas Mangum, Carrie Sinclair Wolcott, ... Wendy Widder. Bellingham, WA: Lexham Press, 2016.

Ryrie, Charles C. *Dr. Ryrie's Articles.* Bellingham, WA: Logos Bible Software, 2010.

Schürer, E. *A History of the Jewish People in the Time of Jesus Christ, First Division.* Vol. 1. Edinburgh: T&T Clark, 1890.

Sick, David H. "The Symposium of the 5,000." *The Journal of Theological Studies* NS, vol. 66, pt. 1 (April 2015): 1.

Simeon, Charles. *Horae Homileticae: Luke XVII to John XII.* Vol. 13. London: Holdsworth and Ball, 1833.

Smith, Dwight Moody. *The Theology of the Gospel of John.* Cambridge: University Press, 1995.

Spence-Jones, H. D. M. "Exodus." *The Pulpit Commentary.* Vol. 1. Peabody, MA: Hendrickson Publishers, 1909.

Spong, John Shelby. *The Fourth Gospel: Tales of a Jewish Mystic.* New York: HarperCollins Publishers, 2013.

Story, Dan. *Defending Your Faith.* Grand Rapids, MI: Kregel Publications, 1997.

Strong, James. *The New Strong's Exhaustive Concordance of the Bible.* Nashville: Thomas Nelson, 1990.

Talbert, Charles H. *Reading John: A Literary and Theological Commentary on the Fourth Gospel and the Johannine Epistles.* Macon, GA: Smyth and Helwys Publishing, 2005.

Thompson, Marianne Meye. "Signs and Faith in the Fourth Gospel." *Bulletin for Biblical Research* 1 (1991): 100.

Thompson, Robin. "Healing at the Pool of Bethesda: A Challenge to Asclepius?" *Bulletin for Biblical Research* 27, no. 1 (2017): 65–84.

Torrey, Reuben Archer. *Difficulties in the Bible: Alleged Errors and Contradictions.* Willow Grove, PA: Woodlawn Electronic Publishing, 1998.

Utley, Robert J. *The Beloved Disciple's Memoirs and Letters: The Gospel of John, I, II, and III John.* Vol. 4. Marshall, TX: Bible Lessons International, 1999.

Vincent, Marvin Richardson. *Word Studies in the New Testament.* Vol. 2. New York: Charles Scribner's Sons, 1887.

Vine, William Edwy. *Vine's Complete Expository Dictionary of Old and New Testament Words.* Nashville: Thomas Nelson, 1996.

Weber, Stuart K. *Matthew.* Vol. 1. Nashville: Broadman and Holman Publishers, 2000.

Wiersbe, Warren W. *The Bible Exposition Commentary.* Vol. 1. Wheaton, IL: Victor Books, 1996.

Winstead, Melton B. "Capernaum." In *The Lexham Bible Dictionary,* eds. John D. Barry, David Bomar, Derek R. Brown, Rachel Klippenstein, Douglas Mangum, Carrie Sinclair Wolcott, … Wendy Widder. Bellingham, WA: Lexham Press, 2016.

Witherington, Ben, III. *The Jesus Quest: The Third Search for the Jew of Nazareth,* 2nd ed. Downers Grove, IL: InterVarsity Press, 1997.

Witherington, Ben, III. *John's Wisdom: A Commentary on the Fourth Gospel.* Louisville, KY: Westminster John Knox Press, 1995.

Wright, Nicholas Thomas. *The Resurrection of the Son of God.* Minneapolis: Fortress Press, 2003.

Solomon Eugene Fields

Personal
Birthplace: Houston, Texas, United States of America, 1956

Education
B.A. Texas Tech University, 1978
M.A. Trinity College of the Bible and Theological Seminary, 2015
D.R.S Trinity College of the Bible and Theological Seminary, 2019

Certificates and Licenses
License to Preach, 1991
Ordination as Minister, 1994
Certificate in Chaplaincy, 2004

Employment
Senior Pastor of St. John Baptist Church, 1994–present

Memberships
Lovely Sunset Baptist District Association: Second Vice President of
    Congress
Lubbock Area Interdenominational Minister's Alliance